Buddhism for Beginners

Gain Inner Peace by Understanding and Implementing Buddhism in Your Life to Increase Your Energy and Reduce Stress and Anxiety

Table of Contents

Introduction
    What Is Buddhism
    The Buddha Philosophy
    Using Buddhism to Live a Better Life

Chapter 1: Life, Death & Spirituality
    The Difference Between Awakened and Enlightened
    Understanding What It Means to Be a Buddhist
    Does Being a Buddhist Mean You Have to Be Vegetarian?
    Do Everything in Moderation
    Do I Have to Convert If I Want to Be a Buddhist?
    Maintaining A Buddhists' Positive Outlook

Chapter 2: What Makes a Buddhist a Buddhist
    What Buddhists Do
    Can Buddhism Help with Anxiety and Depression?
    Understanding the Gestures
        Bhumisparsha
        The Dharmachakra
        The Dhyan
        Vitarka
        Karana
        Uttarabodhi
        Varada
        Anjali
        Vajra

    Abhaya
  The Right Discipline
    The Right Understanding/Right View
    The Right Intention/Thought
    The Right Speech
    The Right Action
    The Right Livelihood
    The Right Effort
    The Right Mindfulness
    The Right Concentration
  Common Practice and Manners When Visiting Buddhist Temples

Chapter 3: Benefits of Buddhism
  Physical Health
  Wealth
  Happiness
  What Does "Enlightenment" Mean?
  The Benefits of Enlightenment and Being Present

Chapter 4: Teachings
  Buddhism and Suffering
  Buddhism and Karma
  Buddhism and Reincarnation, Nirvana and Yoga
  Rituals and Rites
    The First Basic Practice: The Veneration
    The Second Basic Practice: The Monks and Laypersons Exchange
    The Uposatha Ritual
    The Anniversary of the 3 Major Events

   The Pilgrimage

Chapter 5: Practices You Can Implement in Your Life
  A Look at Your Routine as A Buddhist
  A Day in The Life of a Buddhist
  Successful Habits of Buddhist Monks You Can Adopt
    Habit #1 - Decluttering You
    Habit #2 - Decluttering Your Environment
    Habit #3 - Attaining Wisdom from the Elders
    Habit #4 - Listen with Mindfulness, Not Judgment
    Habit #5 - Understanding That Change Is the Only Law
    Habit #6 - Focus Only on One
    Habit #7 - Don't Control What You Cannot
    Habit #8 - Removing Your 3 Poisons

Chapter 6: Mindfulness and Acceptance Techniques for Anxiety and Stress
  Understanding Mindfulness
  Where Do Stress and Anxiety Come From?
  What Buddhists Do to Calm the Mind
    The First Stage: Mindfulness of Anatomy, Body, and Elements
    The Second Stage: Being Mindful Towards Feelings
    The Third Stage: Being Mindful of Consciousness
    The Fourth Stage: Being Mindful of Mental Objects

Chapter 7: The Diet of a Buddhist
  Dietary Regulations in Different Buddhist Sects
  Dietary Restrictions
  Common Ingredients Found in a Buddhist Diet
  Eating Times

Are You Still Considered a Buddhist If You Eat Meat?

Exercising for Good Health

Chapter 8: Meditation

How the Buddhists Do It (Types of Meditation)

The Benefits

Meditation and Prayers Are Different

Meditation's Biggest Challenges

Mastering the Basics: How to Begin to Meditate

How to Perform the Shamatha

The Advanced Meditation Technique that Frees You from Suffering

Chapter 9: What You Didn't Know About Buddhism

5 Things You Didn't Know About Buddhism

1. There's No Official Standard of Buddhism

2. Sometimes Buddha is Depicted Fat, and Sometimes He Is Skinny

3. Buddha Sometimes Has an Acorn on His Head and Here's Why

4. Not All Buddhists Wear Orange and Yellow Robes

5. There Are No Women Buddha's

Amazing Zen Buddhist Stories That Teach Us About Life

Story 1 - Suzuki Roshi's Lesson on Impermanence

Story 2 - The Horse and the Boss

Story 3 - It's Not Always About Following the Rules

Story 4 - When It's Time to Die

Famous People Who Follow Buddhism

The 14th Dalai Lama

Thich Nhat Hanh

Steve Jobs, American Entrepreneur
Adewale Akinnuoye-Agbaje, British Actor
Chow Yun-Fat, Hong Kong Actor
Tina Turner, Retired Singer, Songwriter and Actress
Conclusion
Description

Introduction

The story of Buddha remains the centerpiece of one of the greatest legends ever told. Buddha's life and the events that led to his awakening remains one of the most renowned narratives in the world. This is where the legend of one of the world's major religions begins more than 2,500 years ago in India.

A long time ago, sometime around 563 B.C.E in the foothills of the Himalayas, a Prince was born. His name was Siddhartha, and he lived a life of luxury, wealth and comfort. Born the warrior son of a king and queen, he had everything a young Prince could ask for. However, legend has it that upon his birth, a soothsayer predicted one day the young prince might renounce his life of wealth and privilege. His father, the king, did everything he could to stop that from happening by showering the young prince with many worldly pleasures and luxuries. One day, as a young man, Siddhartha witnessed something on his chariot ride that would change him forever. It was then he saw the first forms of human suffering. Illness, old age, death, misery opened the young Prince's eyes, and from that point on, he grew increasingly discontented with his sheltered, materialistic lifestyle. The stark contrasts between the life he led and the suffering of others that he saw outside the palace walls were something he never got over. It was then he began to realize that all the pleasures and materialism of this world were nothing more than a mask of what true human suffering was like, and he grew increasingly discontented with his sheltered, materialistic lifestyle.

Deeply moved by what he saw outside the palace, this led him to give away everything he owned. Siddhartha was determined to search for enlightenment by abandoning his basic needs. He left his wife and the son he had, and with several teachers in tow, sought severe renunciation in the nearby forest and thus began his period of starvation. Legend says that he became so thin when he was on the brink of near-starvation before he finally realized that this approach was only adding to his suffering, not offering a solution.

Siddhartha was determined to follow the Middle Path because he knew he needed to find a way to balance his rich and impoverished life. As he sat under the pipal tree, he began to seek enlightenment through meditation, fighting off all worldly temptations as he continued to remain focused. After 40 days, he finally reached his ultimate goal of reaching nirvana. Upon achieving enlightenment, Prince Siddhartha became the *Shakyamuni,* who went on to preach this newfound path of salvation to the rest of his followers. To his followers, he became known as Buddha (The Awakened One), Siddhartha Gautama, or Gautama Buddha. Buddhism quickly grew to become one of the most important religions within the Asian region, and today it is practiced by more than 300 million people around the world.

Buddha traveled throughout northeastern India during his time for several decades as he sought to share his experience and teach his followers what he called *The Middle Path*. He shared his philosophy with anyone who was eager and willing to learn, irrespective of their race, caste, or gender. His teachings were so profound and impactful that members of nobility and Brahmins were converted. Until the time of his death in 483 B.C.E, Buddha spent 45 years traveling and teaching his followers.

Although he was the founder, Buddha was not a God. He was an extraordinary man, yes, but a man nonetheless. After his death, small communities of nuns and monks sprung up and devoted themselves to continue his teachings, and these became the first building blocks of the Buddhist religion today.

In India, Buddhism became the state religion around 3rd-century B.C. when a Mauryan Indian emperor known as Ashoka the Great made it so. It was then Buddhist monasteries were first built in the area, and followers were encouraged to take up missionary work. Some followers interpreted the teachings and ideas in different ways, and over the next few centuries, the religion would go to spread beyond India as the philosophies and teachings of Buddhism grew more diverse.

India was invaded by the Huns in the 6th-century, and the invasion saw hundreds of Buddhist monasteries destroyed before the intruders were finally driven out. Buddhism was forced underground once more in the Middle Ages when Islam started gaining momentum and spreading.

What Is Buddhism

Buddhism is now among the world's three major religions, the other two being Islam and Christianity. The religion has assumed several forms throughout the years, but in every form its teachings always attempted to draw inspiration from Buddha's teachings. Buddhist monks and nuns are known as *Bhikkhus*, and upon Buddha's death, they took over the responsibility of spreading his teachings and philosophies. *Bhikkhus,* they adhere to a strict code of conduct and this code includes the code of celibacy.

Buddhism has always been a religion that adopted a more flexible approach to its practice. It stays true to its core teachings, but at the same time, encourages its followers to adapt to the various local ideas and conditions around them, all the while never straying far from its main teachings and philosophy. With its vast geographical expansion combined with its tolerant spirit, Buddhism as a religion today encompasses several traditions, practices, and beliefs. For centuries, it has been a powerful and dominant force within Asia, touching on many different aspects, including mythology lore, arts, morals, social institutions and more. Within the last decade, Buddhism has a stronger foothold and presence outside its Asian origins, and its influence is growing quickly in the Western world.

The focus of Buddhism is to achieve enlightenment, and because of that, followers of the religion do not acknowledge a supreme deity or god. Instead, Buddhists focus on achieving wisdom and inner peace to achieve nirvana. Enlightenment can be achieved when followers utilize meditation, wisdom, and morality. Followers of the religion are encouraged to meditate often to help them "awaken" the truth.

Buddhism is a religion that is tolerant and constantly evolving. Certain scholars believe that Buddhism is not so much a religion, but rather a "spiritual tradition" or way of life. Self-denial and self-indulgence must be avoided. Buddhism believes in the concept of *karma* and *reincarnation*. Followers are free to worship either at home or at temples. Buddhism does not have a fixed symbol of its own. Over the years, several images have evolved to represent Buddhism and its beliefs. Some of these common images include the lotus flower, the Bodhi tree, the *swastika,* and the eight-spoked dharma wheel.

Although Buddhism exists in several forms globally today, three primary types of Buddhism remain prevalent:

- **Tibetan** - Dominant in Tibet, northern India, Nepal, Bhutan, certain areas in Russia and Mongolia.

- ***Theravada*** - Dominant in Burma, Thailand, Cambodia, Laos, and Sri Lanka

- ***Mahayana*** - Dominant in Vietnam, China, Singapore, Japan, Korea and Taiwan.

Each of the three types listed above interprets Buddha's teachings differently, although the differences are slight. Buddhism has also branched out into several subsects, including *Nirvana* and *Zen Buddhism*. Some forms of Buddhism encompass the ideas taken from other philosophies and religions too, including *Taoism*.

Dalai Lama is the title that is bestowed to Tibetan Buddhism's leading monk. Followers believe that the *Dalai Lama* is a reincarnation of a *lama* in the past who agreed to be reborn. 14 *Dalai Lamas* have been recorded so far throughout history.

The Buddha Philosophy

Asking a Buddhist "what they believe" is a hard question to answer. That's because Buddhism has evolved so much in various parts of the world that it is a "family of religions" rather than a single religion alone. Ask a Buddhist what they believe, and you're likely to get a different answer depending on which approach to Buddhism they practice. Essentially, Buddha taught his followers that the dissatisfaction, illness, suffering, aging, and death we experience are all integral components to this thing we call life, but suffering is something we *create* for ourselves through our attachment. When we want things to be done in a certain way, we "suffer" when it doesn't go according to plan because we continue clinging to the expectations we have. All our actions and every thought we have has consequences to it. It will either alleviate your suffering or aggravate it. This cause and effect chain is *karma*.

When he was alive, Buddha taught his followers that kindness, compassion, wisdom, generosity, and patience were some of the most important virtues a person could possess. His teachings are referred to as the *Dharma,* and all Buddhists live by five core moral precepts specifically:

- Do not kill any living thing
- Do not take what has not been given to you
- Do not lie
- Do not abuse alcohol and drugs
- Do not engage in sexual misconduct

Buddha taught his followers many things, but his *most* important philosophies revolve around the *Four Noble Truths* and *Eightfold Path,* which are the fundamental philosophies all followers need to familiarize themselves with to understand the religion.

In the *Four Noble Truths,* the fundamental philosophies center around four aspects, which collectively explain why we suffer as humans and how to overcome it. The four truths are the:

- *Dukkha* - Suffering and the truth behind it
- *Samudaya* - Cause of suffering and the truth behind it
- *Nirhodha* - End of suffering and the truth behind it
- *Magga* - Freeing yourself from suffering and the truth behind this path

To bring an end to life's suffering, Buddha taught his followers that the way to achieve that was through the *Eightfold Path*. Under this path, followers were taught to follow the ideals for achieving wisdom, ethical conduct, and mental discipline that include (in no specific order):

- *Samma Ditthi* - Your right to understanding
- *Samma Sati* - Your right to mindfulness
- *Samma Kammanta* - Your right to action
- *Samma Sankappa* - Your right to thought
- *Samma Ajiva* - Your right to livelihood
- *Samma Vayama* - Your right to effort
- *Samma Samadhi* - Your right to concentration
- *Samma Vaca* - Your right to speech

Several scriptures and texts are revered by Buddhists, and the most important ones include:

- **The *Sutras*** - These are a collection of more than 2,000 sutras that contained the sacred teachings embraced by the Mahayana Buddhists.

- **The *Tipitaka*** - These are known as the "three baskets" texts and are thought to be a collection of some of Buddhism's earliest writings.

- **The Book of the Dead** - The stages of human death is described in vivid detail in these Tibetan texts.

Using Buddhism to Live a Better Life

The word Buddhism conjures images of men donning orange and yellow robes sitting peacefully as they either meditate or chant mantra for inner peace. We envision temples or peaceful settings with the chime of soft bells in the background. But that's a vision best left in Hollywood. In reality, Buddhism is about spirituality and living your life in a way that shows your commitment, dedication, and live to be better and live better. Buddhism and its many teachings can easily be infused into our daily activities, with many practitioners already doing so to live a better life.

If you had to answer the question *why did you choose to go into Buddhism,* what would your answer be? Was it because you sought inner peace? More tranquility amid the chaos of your busy life? That you were searching for balance for happiness? The beautiful thing about this religion is that unlike many other religions out there, the emphasis is less on the important role Gods and deities play and more about using the teachings to transform the essence of your life for the better. No matter what your reason may be for beginning this journey, Buddhism can always be used in several ways to live a better life, and this is where you begin:

- **Live Simple, Live Free** - Happiness lies in simplicity. Too much of our lives are dictated by our desires, wants and needs. We want the newest car, the latest phone, new shoes, new clothes. The wants never end, and they never will unless you *choose* to cut ties with your needs and desires. Craving for material goods is not the Buddhist way, and when you learn to be grateful for the simple things in life, that's when true happiness and contentment begin.

- **Never Stop Learning** - Buddhism's teachings believe that the more you learn, the closer you to achieving enlightenment. Knowledge is something we must always thirst for, and this practice teaches us to never become complacent enough to believe we have learned enough.

- **Adopt the Right View** - Under the *Eightfold Path*, Buddhists are taught to understand that reality is something temporary. It is not a definitive truth. The suffering you go through is only temporary; it is not your reality. Adopting this mindset keeps you persistent and focused on your goals, and you're less likely to give up in the face of challenges.

- **Avoid Arguments** - Buddha reminded his followers that we have only a short time on this earth, and knowing this, we would be foolish to waste that time on arguments that are only temporary. Buddhism preaches forgiveness and tolerance, and to not harbor hatred even for those who have wronged us, so you don't deprive yourself of inner peace. Forget the argument with your colleague, friend, family, or stranger. Forgive and move on for it is simply not worth carrying that anger around with you.

- **Learning to Let Go** - Buddha believed that when we finally learn how to let go from everything that is holding you back, you're free to live your life and find your spiritual path. How many times has holding back or holding on to what you should have let go of long ago stopped you from being happy? From being free? Let it go.

There are plenty of books on this subject on the market, thanks again for choosing this one! Every effort was made to ensure it is full of as much useful information as possible; please enjoy!

Chapter 1: Life, Death & Spirituality

When we think of Buddhism, we often associate it with peace, meditation, and being enlightened. But there is more to being a Buddhist than merely meditating and living a peaceful, contented life.

The Difference Between Awakened and Enlightened

Even Buddhists tend to use these two words interchangeably. Essentially, they mean the same thing. There's only a slight difference between them. Enlightenment is an experience and an understanding of your reality. You understand the world you live in as it is without muddying the waters with your perception, ideas, beliefs, and concepts.

Awakened, however, means you begin to see life as it unfolds. The path to awakening involves several steps before you reach the final step where a radical shift in your perspective takes place (also when enlightenment happens). There is a paradoxical statement used by Zen Buddhists, which they use to meditate upon. This statement is simple, yet profound, and it says: *Awakening can only be attained when you enter through the gateless gate.* What this is meant to teach us is that as long as there is a gate, you cannot enter into the awakened state. Only *when you realize there is no gate,* that's the moment you realize you've been in the awakened state all the along. The only thing that was holding you back from seeing this was the mistaken belief that you were *outside the gate.* What this statement is trying to tell us is that we don't need to become awakened. Everything we need to be present is already within us right now.

Understanding What It Means to Be a Buddhist

If Buddhism could be summarized into one key teaching, that teaching would be about the nature of suffering and how to end that suffering. One of Buddha's first teachings, after he reached his enlightened state, was about the *Four Noble Truths* that were mentioned at the start of this book. Think of the *Four Noble Truths* in medical terms. In this context, Buddha is the doctor, and he diagnosed that the problem is suffering. He has also identified the causes of this suffering and identified the prognosis before finally prescribing us with a cure. That cure is the *Four Noble Truths,* the essence of what it means to be a Buddhist. These four truths form the core of all other Buddhist teachings, traditions and pathways and it encompasses all we need to know about life, death, and spirituality.

There is also a certain lifestyle that goes with being a Buddhist, and it is associated with nonviolence and living a life that is free from material longing. Buddhism may not have a list of rules like a lot of other religions or a certain deity that it reveres, but what it has instead is five basic precepts that most practicing Buddhists strive to live by. These precepts are not a set of rules like the Ten Commandments, for example, but rather they are what you might call recommendations. A guide pointing out the steps needed to live a more harmonious life. Practicing Buddhists believe that these precepts form the pathway towards enlightenment since it is believed that anyone who lives by these precepts is already enlightened anyway.

The five precepts of what it means to be a Buddhist are:

- **You Do Not Take a Life** - This is *the most* absolute teaching in Buddhism. It is interpreted differently from one person and one tradition to another. Not taking a life may form the precept of some people's stance on capital punishment, abortion, or the killing of animals (even insects). To weight the consequences of their actions, Buddhists are encouraged to reflect on whether their actions are motivated by hatred, greed, wisdom, compassion, or kindness. The *intention* behind the action is the defining difference. One example to illustrate this point would be if you or your family were under attack that threatened your very lives. In this case, you might have no other choice but to take a life to save your own. If the killing is done without anger or hatred, it may still be interpreted that you're living in accordance with the precept.

- **You Do Not Spread False Speech** - Telling lies is spreading false speech. Speech that is spread out of greed, hatred, and ignorance is false speech. Intentionally misleading others with your communication is false speech. False speech is not confined to merely telling a lie. Being a Buddhist means you need to examine the impact of your words and choose your words wisely because once spoken out loud, they can never be taken back again. Your words have the power to cause great harm to yourself an another. Negative thoughts and words that you use on yourself have the power to destroy your confidence and your self-esteem, making it difficult to love yourself and be happy with who you are. Negative thoughts and words used on another can be just as harmful and malevolent when it causes them a great deal of pain. Many suicide cases these days among young people are a direct result of bullying, and it is a prime example of what false speech can do. It can destroy lives and lead others to take their own lives when the suffering becomes too much to bear.

- **You Do Not Take What Is Not Given** - This one doesn't talk about stealing alone. It encompasses everything from your motivation to understanding how your actions are going to impact others. If an idea at work was not yours, to begin with, you do not take credit for it. When you did not put in the hard work for it, do not take credit for something your team members did. When you don't take what does not belong to you, there is happiness to be found in that action. Be happy knowing that what you have now was attained without causing harm to another. That is was attained without the need to steal. Peace and joy are attainable when you live a life with no remorse.

- **You Do Not Engage in Sexual Misconduct** - This one is interpreted and understood differently depending on the school of Buddhism that is understanding it. The monks and nuns of the Theravada Buddhists, for instance, remain celibate. Other schools of Buddhism, like the *Jodo Shinshu* in Japan, view marriage as an acceptable thing for its clergy members. "Misconduct" is interpreted based on societal views and the culture of different practitioners. Sexual exploitation would be deemed misconduct, as would sex that is not consensual. As with the other precepts, you need to make your own judgment based on how your actions are going to impact another.

- **You Do Not Engage in Intoxicants That Cloud Your Mind** - Some schools of Buddhism take this precept to mean that they must stay away from intoxicating substances like drugs and alcohol at all costs. An intoxicant is anything that is going to prevent your mind from thinking clearly and making sound decisions. Anything that is going to alter your perception and prevent your ability to make rational judgments. An intoxicating substance these days could even refer to social media where false truths are being spread all the time. If we were not careful, we could easily be swayed by many of the false truths we are exposed to.

Does Being a Buddhist Mean You Have to Be Vegetarian?

Buddha did not make it a strict law for his followers to be vegetarians. While he did not condone the act of taking a life, he also taught his followers to be gracious and accept any food that was offered to them, meat included. It is entirely up to the practitioner if you want to be a vegetarian or not. Some schools of Buddhism do practice vegetarianism; others do not. The freedom of choice is yours, and it is up to you to decide if being a vegetarian is going to align with your life's circumstances.

Do Everything in Moderation

Buddhism is a peaceful religion, and it places a lot of emphasis on avoiding any unnecessary suffering on yourself or others. This explains why there are no fixed rules that you absolutely must follow, no laws that dictate what you should or should not do. Some people might be happy following certain rules, while others find it a great cause of unhappiness (suffering). To be a Buddhist is to gain greater insight into the nature of your mind, and to understand what causes your happiness and misery.

Do everything in moderation, and you will be happy. If the action you take is not going to negatively impact yourself or others around you, there's no reason to hold back if it is an action you want to take. The key is to find balance and not veer towards one extreme or the other. To be a Buddhist means to spend a lot of time in self-reflection to arrive at decisions, thoughts, and actions that are going to have the best overall outcome for everyone involved.

Do I Have to Convert If I Want to Be a Buddhist?

That is entirely up to you as once again; it comes back to your freedom of choice. Buddhism is not a religion based on force, and since it is not proselytizing, it is not focused or interested in forcing anyone to convert. You can, if you want to, but you are the only one who can make that choice. Living life as a Buddhist is only going to be effective if the five precepts mentioned above are teachings that make sense to you. Teachings that you can see yourself living by each day with ease. Buddhism is a religion for everyone, regardless of gender or race. If you decide that Buddhism is the right path for you and this is the journey you need to take for your own benefit, do it.

If you do decide that you want to become a Buddhist, you can take refuge in what Buddhists call *The Three Jewels* or the *Three Refuges*. These three elements are:

- The Buddha
- The *Dharma* (the teachings)
- The *Sangha* (the community)

You will find *The Three Jewels* are a formal ceremony that is conducted in Buddhist temples. If you don't go to a temple, *The Three Jewels* are easily done anywhere you are. All you need to do is simply recite: *I take refuge in the Buddha, the Dharma, and the Sangha.*

Maintaining A Buddhists' Positive Outlook

The Buddhists believe that good and evil are not forces that are inherent in the universe. Rather, the concept of good and evil is a state of mind that exists within us. Buddhism teaches us to look inside ourselves for the answers that we seek. What we say, think, and do, our minds are the source of what we perceive to be bad or evil. Likewise, to look at life in a positive way, the first place to begin would be within your mind. Understanding that you are responsible for your own good and evil creates a greater sense of responsibility. It teaches us that we are accountable for every thought, every word, and every action we put out there in the world.

Negative influences like ignorance, greed, and hatred are what Buddhism calls *"The Three Poisons."* These three factors consistently drive us to look externally and lead us to believe that happiness is external. We are misled into believing that to be happy, we must avoid suffering. Buddhist teachings gently point out that lasting happiness can never be attained when you continue chasing power, money, and fame. Material things are not meant to last. If it were the source of happiness, Buddha would never have abandoned his life of wealth all those centuries ago. He believed that the pursuit of happiness begins with an understanding of *what* causes your suffering. The *root* cause. Maintaining a positive outlook in life begins with a daily practice of being mindful of your thoughts. One of the central tenets of this practice is that our emotions are not unchangeable. Buddha himself once said: *We are what we think, and everything that happens is because of our thoughts. Our thoughts make the world.*

This simple philosophy reminds us that positivity and happiness must start within our minds. To challenge your negative thoughts by replacing them with positive ones. Buddhists use meditation is one approach to detach themselves from their thoughts, and meditation has proven time and time again what an effective tool it can be to help us practice mindful awareness. Buddhists teachings have long held the answer to happiness, and these key principles will help you get started on your journey to transforming your thoughts into positive ones:

- **Practice Mindfulness** - It is a core Buddhist belief that when we are mindful, we remain present and aware of our surroundings. We pay attention to what's happening *now* rather than fixating on events of the past or future. Studies have shown that those who practice mindfulness show a significant increase in their levels of happiness, supporting what Buddhism has been teaching its followers all along: *When your mind is calm and pure, only then will wisdom emerge.*

- **Don't Compare** - Buddhists live by many principles, and one of them being that all living things are created equal. The belief is that all of us are connected, and comparing yourself to another is only causing you greater suffering. Being superior or inferior does not exist in Buddhism.

- **Abandon the Chase for Money** - Buddha gave up his life of material wealth because he realized that materialism would never bring happiness. That is a false refuge many of us let ourselves believe in. Abandon the chase for money, and immerse yourself in feeling grateful for everything that you have in your life now. You are blessed in many ways, and once you become mindful of this, it is not difficult to remain positive.

- **Live with Gratitude** - A heart that is truly full and grateful could never be unhappy. Buddha once said that gratitude was the "highest protection" against every form of unhappiness our mind can conjure. Our minds are sometimes the cause of our greatest suffering, and we must counter that with a heart that is full and grateful instead. Mindfulness helps us remain focused and appreciative of what we have in the present, which makes it easier to stay positive.

- **Love Unconditionally** - Buddhist teachings encourage us to love without attachment. This means that we should freely love others without expecting anything in return. We don't need to change them, and we don't need to control them. All we need to do is love them. Buddha believed that kind words, beneficial help, generosity, and being consistent were the ties that bound us all together. There's more than enough research out there too that shows those who have good relationships in their lives are happier people.

- **Practice *Dana*** - It means giving. Being generous and giving can be done in more ways than just money and material belongings. Buddhist teachings tell us that there is a benefit in the giving of items that are less tangible, too, like your support, time, and money for example.

Chapter 2: What Makes a Buddhist a Buddhist

Buddhists are generally happy people because of the way of life they have chosen to follow. Deciding to become a Buddhist, though, does not mean that everything is going to magically fall into place and that all your problems will sort themselves out overnight but it will make a tremendous difference in the way you overcome adversity in life.

So how is life going to be different as a Buddhist? What *makes you a Buddhist?*

What Buddhists Do

As a Buddhist, the biggest change you are going to encounter is a change in your possession. You don't need to wear special clothes to show the world you're a Buddhist, and neither do you have to change your eating habits. You don't have to give away all your belongings like Siddhartha did because we still need them to survive and function every day. What makes a person a Buddhist is the change in their perception. Buddhists learn to see that obstacles and challenges are not to be taken seriously because they don't last, and that life around us is full of potential to make each day a better one. A change in mindset sounds easy enough, but it is anything but easy.

Buddhists begin shifting their mindset through Siddhartha's teachings and with the help of meditation and mindfulness. Through mindfulness, they slowly lift the veil that we all wear, which sometimes stops us from seeing things for what they are. What Buddha left behind as part of his legacy was a treasury full of advice. Each tradition places a different emphasis on the various aspects of Buddhism. Laypeople, nuns, and monks have very different lifestyles when it comes to living out the teachings.

To become a Buddhist, you need to do what they do, and that means you need to:

- Begin accepting responsibility for shaping your reality through your thoughts and actions. To be accountable and understand that if you suffer, it is because your thoughts and actions have made it so in some way.
- Understand the concept of karma, cause, and effect are real. What you create today will cause your situation tomorrow.
- Understand that your thoughts and judgments bring about attitudes and habits that will either limit you or free you.
- Develop a set of values you can trust. To take refuge in the *Dharma, Sangha, and Lama* in times of doubt.
- Practice meditation to become enlightened. The goal strived for in all Buddhist practices and teachings is to reach enlightenment. Buddha taught all his followers that *anyone* can achieve enlightenment, and his teachings are there to help us along the path to that goal.

Can Buddhism Help with Anxiety and Depression?

Being interested in Buddhism and its teachings does not necessarily mean you need to convert to benefit from its wisdom and philosophy. Buddhism can be of great help to you, even if you're only interested in being happier. If you're dealing with anxiety and depression, the path to happiness and feeling like your old self again can feel like an impossible quest. Anxiety happens when our imagination runs away with us, and our mind goes into overdrive, conjuring up scenarios that cause a great deal of stress. Even if half the time these scenarios are imagined, it doesn't stop us from feeling worried about the difficulties that don't exist. Enter Buddhism and its mindful meditation practice that helps us feel grounded once more by helping us slow our thoughts when they spiral out of control.

A Buddhist's approach to anxiety is to welcome it like an old friend instead of trying to resist it. Buddha taught his followers about the two arrows in life. The first arrow represents emotions like depression and anxiety. The second arrow is the way *you feel about these feelings*. About whether you feel angry, sad, or resentful that you're dealing with anxiety and depression. Buddhism teaches its followers that we must avoid the second arrow to minimize the suffering we feel, and we do that by following the Buddhist way of life.

Understanding the Gestures

Images and depictions of Buddha display him with a particular hand gesture. These hand gestures are known as *Mudras* in Sanskrit, and this symbolic gesture is an iconic representational image of Buddha. *Mudras* are commonly depicted in Buddhist art, not just on statues of Buddha alone. The *Mudras* are specific and meant to invoke a certain state of mind. Buddha is commonly depicted with the *Mudra* where his hands are folded in his lap, and this image is meant to signify meditation. Other statues of Buddha depict him with the *Mudra,* where he has one palm held up and facing outwards to signify reassurance. Statues where his open palm is facing downwards, however, are meant to represent generosity.

Buddhist art is intertwined with that of Hindu art sculptures. Each image or depiction is a symbolic representation of divinity. Some of the common hand gestures you'll come across in Buddhism include the following:

Bhumisparsha

This gesture is also called "touching the Earth." In this *Mudra,* your right hand will be held above your right knee. You will then reach towards the ground with your palm facing inwards while attempting to touch the lotus throne. The *Bhumisparsha* is thought to be representational of the moment when Buddha became the Awakened One, and the earth, he claimed, was the only witness of his moment of enlightenment.

Image Source: Jagran Josh

The Dharmachakra

This *Mudra* is also known as the *"Teaching of the Wheel of Dharma"* gesture. Both hands will be held against your chest in this move, with the left hand faced inward. The left hand will be covering the right, which should be facing outward. This gesture is believed to be one of the most important gestures during Buddha's life. He performed this gesture when he gave his first sermon in Sarnath. This sermon was the first-time Buddha began imparting his wisdom after achieving enlightenment.

Image Source: Jagran Josh

The Dhyan

Samadhi or *Yoga* are alternative names given to this *Mudra*. Both hands should be placed on your lap for this move. You will then place your right hand on the left with your fingers stretched. Your thumbs should be facing up. The rest of your fingers on both hands should be resting on each other. This gesture is a common characteristic among the Dhyani Buddha Amitabh, the Medicine Buddha, and the Buddha Shakyamuni.

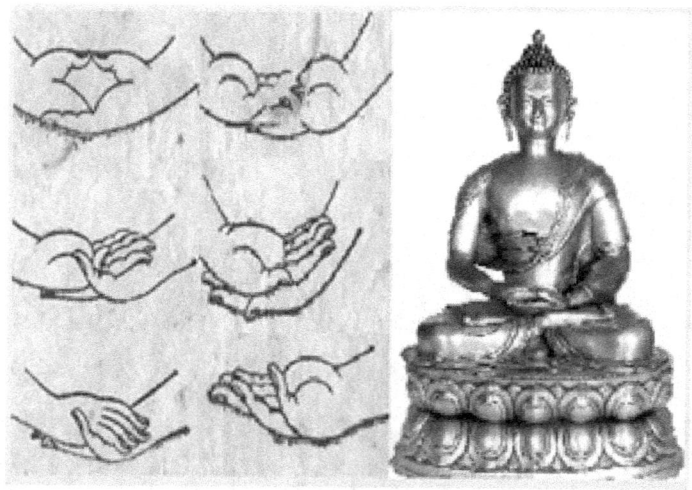

Image Source: Jagran Josh

Vitarka

By joining the tips of your thumb and index finger as your other fingers remain straight, you're performing the *Vitarka* gesture. This *Mudra* signals the transmission and the discussion of Buddha's teachings.

Image Source: Jagran Josh

Karana

Your index and pinky finger will be raised for this gesture, folding the other fingers. The *Karana* is thought to be a symbolic gesture that wards of evil, negative thoughts, and minimize the impact of illnesses.

Image Source: Jagran Josh

Uttarabodhi

Supreme enlightenment is depicted using the *Uttarabodhi* gesture. It is a symbolic *Mudra* that shows you're connecting yourself to the universe's energy. Both hands will be placed at your heart for this gesture. Your index fingers should be touching each other and pointed upwards. The remaining fingers will be intertwined.

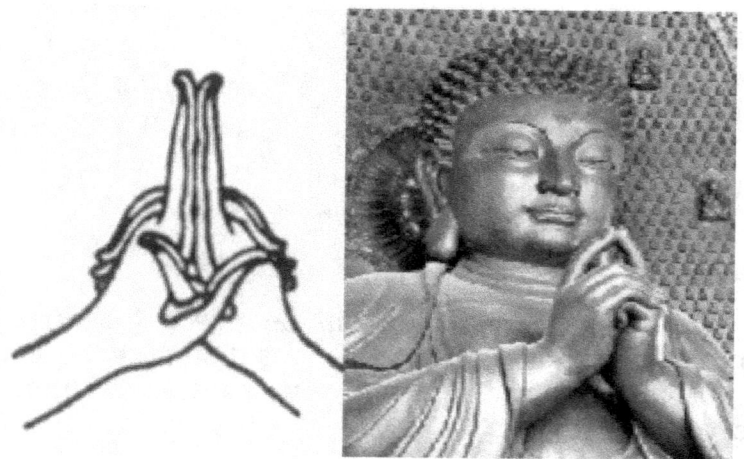

Image Source: Jagran Josh

Varada

Sincerity, offering, compassion, welcome, giving, and charity are what the *Varada* represents. In this gesture, your right palm will face forward as your fingers extend. The left palm will be placed at the omphalos with your fingers extended.

Image Source: Jagran Josh

Anjali

Hridayanjali and *Namaskara* are other terms that this *Mudra* goes by. The *Anjali* is meant to represent adoration, greeting, and prayer. To perform this move, both your palms should be pressed together. They should be positioned near your heart center as your thumbs rest lightly on your sternum.

Image Source: Jagran Josh

Vajra

The *Vajra* is symbolic of the five elements (water, air, metal, fire, and earth). To perform this gesture, the forefinger on your left hand is going to be raised while the right fist encloses this finger.

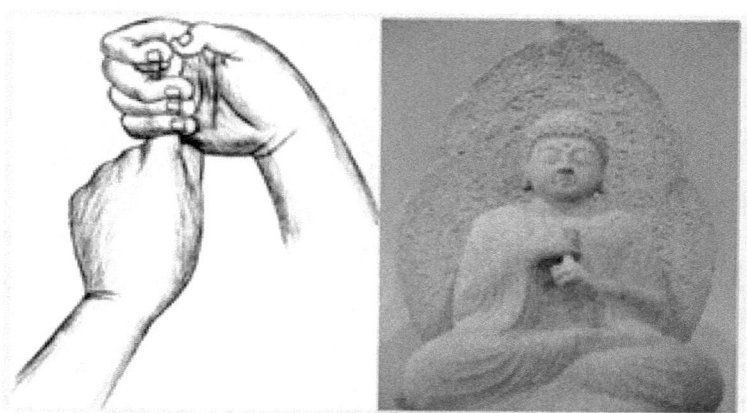

Image Source: Jagran Josh

Abhaya

This gesture could either represent fearlessness or dispelling fear, blessings, protection, benevolence, and peace. Your right hand will be raised to shoulder height for this *Mudra*. Your arm will be bent as you raise your hand, and your palm should face outward. Your left hand will be hanging below your right. The Dhyani Buddha Amoghasiddhi and the Buddha Shakyamuni characteristically use this gesture.

Image Source: Jagran Josh

The Right Discipline

The *Noble Eightfold Path* in Buddhism talks about the eight *right* discipline practices that will lead to liberation from suffering. In the early days of Buddhism, these practices began with an understanding that the body and mind work in a corrupted way, and it is through the *Noble Eightfold Path* that we bring an end to our suffering.

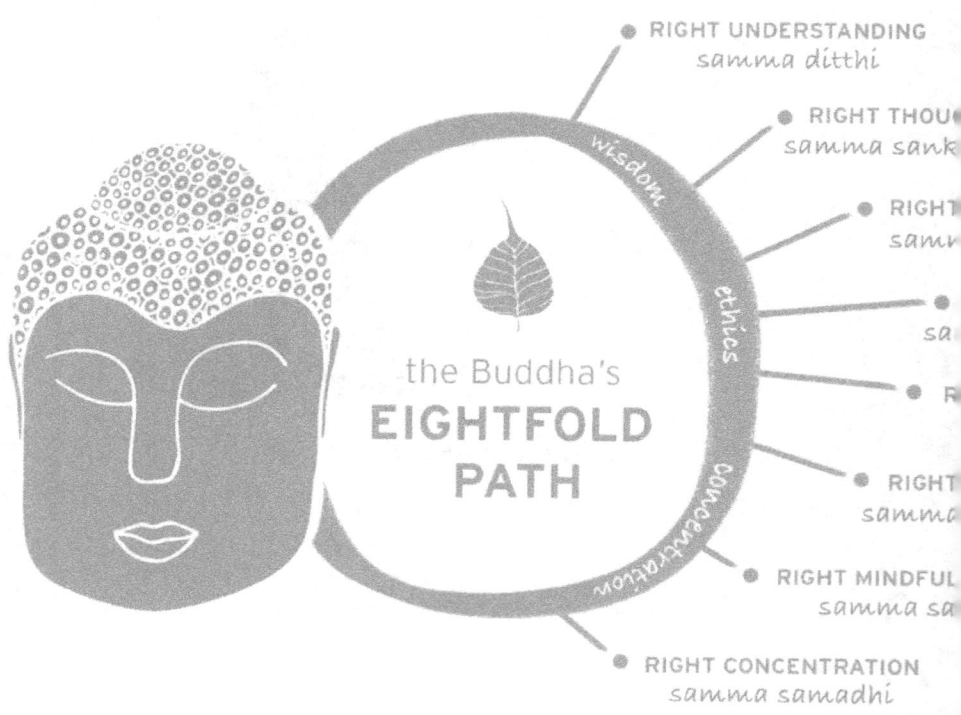

Image Source: Tricycle.org

Symbolically in Buddhism, this *Noble Eightfold Path* is represented using the *Dharma Wheel* with eight spokes sticking out of the wheel. Each spoke represents each of the eight elements.

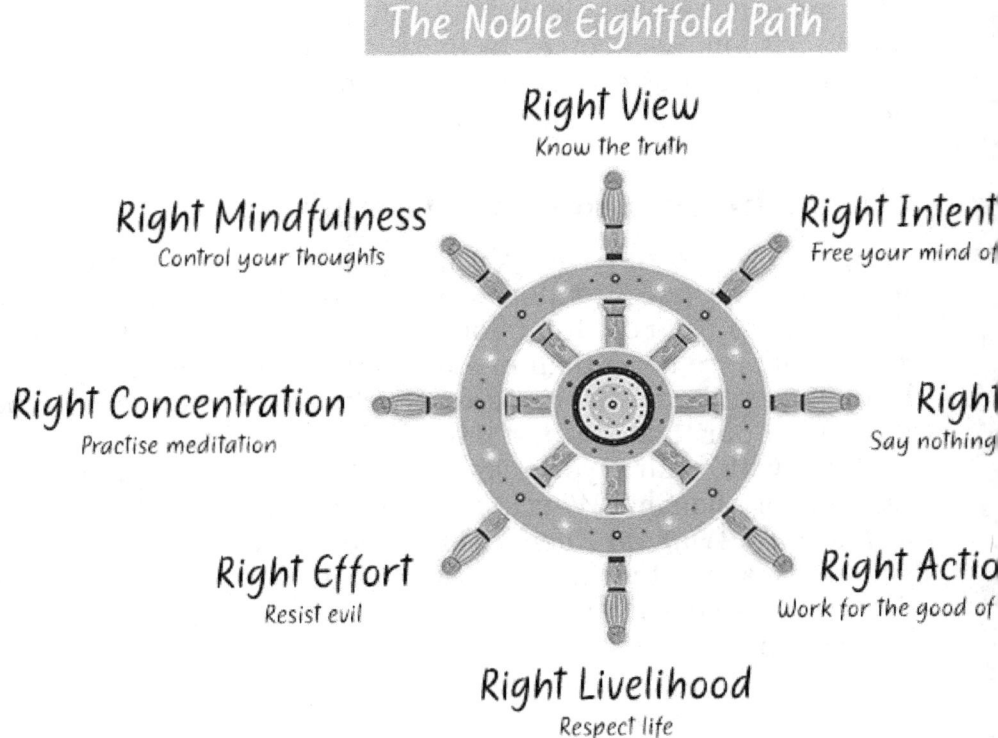

Image Source: Mammoth Memory

The Right Understanding

The *Right Understanding* is about recognizing that we might not see our reality for what it is. When you walk out of your house and encounter a coiled hose, you mistake it for a snake. That is *not your reality* because it is not a snake. Instead, what you're experiencing is a *picture of that reality* in your mind. You immediately react as if it was a snake, feeling frightened, startled and turned around ready to run. Yet, the reality is, there is no snake. Wisdom happens when you stop to assess your situation properly only to realize that it was a hose, and not a snake. This path is here to help remind us that we must continually seek out wisdom to continue learning, so we always have the wisdom we need to see the world for what it is.

Wisdom is not always about piling on more knowledge into your brain. Wisdom also comes in the form of unlearning the ideas and concepts you've been carrying around all along that have held you back from seeing your reality.

The Right Intention and Thought

To minimize the suffering you feel, you must be aware of your intentions. To pay attention to the thoughts you have and the things you say and do. Intentions born out of anger and hate will cause you more harm than intentions that stem from happiness, love, and gratitude. Behaving reactively makes it difficult to be mindful of our thoughts and intentions. This takes practice, and it starts with asking yourself, *"Why?"* when you experience a reaction or thought. *Why am I experiencing this? Why am I feeling this? Why am I being kind?* The *"Why?"* makes you stop and think about the intention behind it. When you're able to determine what your intentions are, you speak, think, and act with caution.

The Right Speech

A harmonious, happy, and peaceful life begins with the way we communicate. Humans, as social creatures, rely on communication as part of our survival function. Not a day goes by when we don't communicate with at least one person throughout the day. *The Right Speech* teaches us to be mindful that our words and speech do not cause any harm. Lying, gossiping, spreading malicious opinions, offering compliments you're not sincere about is not the path towards harmony and happiness. *The Right Speech* is about being genuine and sincere when you communicate. Again, think about the intention behind it. The speech might not always be pleasant or easy to hear, but if there is genuine intent behind its purpose to help another, that's okay.

The Right Action

When you do what is necessary given your current situation, that's the *Right Action*. The pathway serves as a guideline to help us behave appropriately in the situations we find ourselves in. Living by a set moral code is difficult because morals evolve and change over time. Morals differ based on culture, and sometimes adhering to the code is not the right action to take at that time and place.

The Right Livelihood

The Right Livelihood looks at the way you make your living and how you interact with other people while you do your job. It encourages its followers to think about whether what you're doing for your livelihood is doing more harm than good. Buddhism and its teachings are beyond being defined by your career. A doctor may do good in his livelihood, but if he takes bribes from pharmaceutical companies to advocate one drug over another, that does not make it right either. We need to make a judgment call and ask ourselves: *Am I doing more harm than good in my livelihood?*

The Right Effort

This path talks about the effort you've put into trying to practice the other paths under the *Noble Eightfold*. It focused on the effort you put in to inflict positive change in your life. Without effort, no real progress can be made. To learn a new skill takes effort. To instill new habits in your life takes effort. To be a better person takes effort. Essentially, the right effort is about putting in the time and work needed to make your life better per the teachings of Buddhism. Without effort, there can be no enlightenment.

The Right Mindfulness

Mindfulness comes back to our ability to pay attention, regardless of whether you're meditating or going about your daily routine. Mindfulness is the key to staying grounded in the present. *The Right Mindfulness* teaches us that when we are aware and present, any given moment is a moment we are capable of contentment. Being content and happy with what you have nourishes feelings of happiness.

The Right Concentration

Your ability to focus your mind entirely on one thing is the *Right Concentration*. The frequent meditation that Buddhists engage in is a wonderful tool that helps strengthen their ability to concentrate. Being mindful also helps with this, and it prevents us from being easily distracted. Distractions are all around us, from the chime of our mobile devices to the advertisements that flood our newsfeed when we log onto social media. Distractions stop us from seeing reality as it is, and once we stop to pay attention, we start to realize what truly matters to our happiness.

Common Practice and Manners When Visiting Buddhist Temples

Buddhism can be practiced at home or at the temples. As a new Buddhist, visiting these temples can seem like an intimating prospect, but there's no need to worry provided you follow their rules and common etiquette. Buddhism welcomes one and all as long as visitors and newcomers remain mindful and respectful of the rules:

- Be respectful in temples by turning off distractions like your mobile phones.

- Remove your shoes before you enter.

- Talk in low voices so as not to disturb those who are meditating and avoid inappropriate conversation.

- It is respectful to cover your shoulders when in a temple and to wear long pants rather than shorts.

- Avoid touching, sitting nearby, or even climbing the raised platform where the Buddha statue is.

- If you want to take pictures, you should ask for permission. Avoid taking pictures during worship.

- Standing up when monks or nuns enter the room is considered a sign of respect and good manners.

Chapter 3: Benefits of Buddhism

It is amazing how this calm, peaceful, and tranquil religion can enhance several facets of our lives in the simplest of ways. There are no major upheavals needed, no drastic changes, no need to completely transform for you are overnight by forcing yourself to become someone you know deep down you are not. The transition towards a better life through Buddhism is gradual, and none of the changes are going to force you to do anything you're not comfortable with.

A consistent theme in Buddhism is to minimize the suffering in our lives, and this includes the suffering we create for ourselves. With every change comes a choice. The decision about whether to carry out this change or not is entirely in your hands. Nothing is forced; nothing is mandatory. It is about what is going to work best for you. A benefit can only *be beneficial* if you are happy with not only the process but the outcome too.

Physical Health

Buddhism believes that illnesses are inevitable, like growing old and eventually dying one day. It is unavoidable, and at some point, in our lives, we are bound to fall sick. While the normal reaction to physical pain and suffering is to avoid it at all costs where possible, Buddhists are taught to mindfully accept their suffering and endure it. Within its teachings lies the notion that sometimes sickness and pain are an opportunity to cultivate a stronger, healthier mindset where patience and tolerance become our strengths. What holds spiritual value in the Buddhist tradition is *not the illness* itself, but rather the *way we respond* to it.

Buddha did not condone the mistreatment of the body and mind. His teachings and practices were meant to benefit us, to see the body as a valuable medium where indispensable good health can be used to maximize our spiritual development. Meditation has always been a core part of a Buddhist's practice because of the benefits it affords in addressing physical illness. When it comes to healing and good health, the emphasis and teachings of this religion have always been rooted in spirituality and the teachings of the Medicine Buddha.

The Medicine Buddha, also known as *Bhaisajyaguru,* is depicted as a healer who cures both physical and mental suffering and disease. In the Mahayana Buddhist texts, the Medicine Buddha is depicted sitting down with his right hand raised in the *Vadra mudra* gesture while his left hand is resting on his lap while holding onto a jar of medicine. Illustrations of the Medicine Buddha show him being surrounded by innumerable sages and all sorts of healing plants. The sutras state that when the future Medicine Buddha was following the *Bodhisattva* path, he vowed to do these 12 things when he attained enlightenment. The 12 vows he took were that:

1. His body would shine with a bright, dazzling light, and this light would be responsible for illuminating innumerable worlds.
2. His body, now pure and radiant, would serve as a light for those who dwell in darkness.
3. Sentient beings will be supplied with material needs.
4. He will guide those who are on the deviant path to find their way back to the Great Vehicle (also known as the Mahayana).
5. Innumerable beings will be enabled to keep the Precepts.
6. Physical affliction will be cured so all beings could live life able-bodies.
7. Those who were sick and with no family will be given healing and a family to help look after them.
8. Women who were unhappy as they were could become men.
9. All beings will be liberated from the bonds of "exterior" sects and the nets of demons.

10. Those imprisoned and in danger of execution will be free of suffering and worry.
11. Those who were desperate for some food and drink will be satiated.
12. Those who were without clothes, suffering in the cold and heat, poor and battling stinging insects will be given garments and comfortable surroundings.

Based on the sutra, Buddha himself declared that *Bhaisajyaguru* will have tremendous healing powers. Buddhists in Japan, China, and Tibet who are devoted to the *Bhaisajyaguru* have acted on behalf of those who are afflicted with illness for centuries.

Wealth

Buddhists view excessive wealth as a source of suffering and attachment. Having so much wealth creates a fear within us of losing that wealth, which then causes suffering. However, wealth itself is not intrinsically bad, and it doesn't mean that the wealthy can't attain enlightenment. On the contrary, being rich puts you in a privileged position to put into practice the other teachings of this religion, especially the teachings of generosity. Wealth is not a problem if it is obtained in an honest, fair, and just manner and used for the benefit of others in your society. Giving compassionately to those who need it is a virtuous thing to do.

In the *Right Livelihood* discipline, there are benefits that can be obtained from wealth. The story of Anathapindika is one such story about the benefits of wealth according to the Buddhist way of life. Anathapindika lived during the time of Buddha and was a wealthy banker and merchant. He was born Sudatta, but given the nickname Anathapindika because of his generosity towards giving to those in need. The name Anathapindika translates to mean *"the one who gives alms to the helpless."* When Anathapindika arrived to see the Blessed One, he bowed and sat on the side. While he sat, the Blessed One asked him: *There are five benefits obtained from wealth. What are they?"*.

- **The First Benefit** - Those who have amassed wealth by their own strength and righteous gain can give themselves pleasure and satisfaction. Wealth earned through the strength of hard work makes him a provider. He can, therefore, provide for himself, his family, and his helpers and maintain pleasure and satisfaction. He has a right to maintain this pleasure by virtue of his hard work.

- **The Second Benefit** - Furthermore, when wealth is earned through his own strength and by the hard work and sweat of his brow and gained in a righteous manner, the wealthy can provide for his friends and associates with satisfaction and pleasure.

- **The Third Benefit** - Wealth obtained righteously through his hard work, and enterprise keeps calamities at bay. Calamities from thieves, fire, flood, kings, and hateful heirs are warded off so the wealthy may be kept safe.

- **The Fourth Benefit** - When wealth is earned through his own strength and by the hard work and sweat of his brow and gained in a righteous manner, the wealthy one can perform the five oblations. The five oblations are done to relatives and guests, kings and devas, and the dead.

- **The Fifth Benefit** - When wealth is earned through his own strength and by the hard work and sweat of his brow and gained in a righteous manner, the wealthy one can institute offerings that are of supreme aim and heavenly that result in happiness, giving to priests and contemplatives who abstain from heedlessness and intoxication and who do all things with humility and patience, who each tame themselves and restrain themselves, and each taking themselves to Unbinding.

Happiness

The Buddhism practiced by Tibetan monks can teach us a lot about happiness. The tradition of this religion has always emphasized mindfulness and compassion to live better lives, among other things. Buddhists believe that to be happy; we need to combine loving-kindness with mindfulness, both of which can be obtained through meditation. Contemplative practices like these help support the development of a greater, conscious state. Buddhism teaches its followers that the path to happiness lies in:

- **Practicing Compassion Always** - A lot of spiritual traditions in the East have some form of loving-kindness practice embedded into it. In Buddhism, loving-kindness is attained through *mettā bhāvanā* meditation. The form of meditation practices sending kindness to yourself, to the people you loved, to the members of your community, to the people you dislike, and all other beings in this world. Tibetan monks practice the *tonglen,* and through this practice, they breathe in suffering and exhale happiness so that pain is reduced and peace is distributed to all beings. Emory University's 2012 study does suggest that training ourselves to practice compassion the way the Tibetans do could potentially boost empathy, while other studies suggest that the loving-kindness mediation could foster positive relationships and enhance our feelings of positivity over time.

- **Being Part of a Supportive Community** - Building happiness is a difficult task to undertake alone, which is why Buddhism believes that being part of a community is an important criterion for living a happy life and a purposeful life. To have a loving, supportive community and to feel a sense of belonging is an inherent need within us all, and to be part of a supportive community is one of the main ingredients needed to be happy.

- **Not Being Afraid of Death** - When faced with the prospect of something unpleasant like death, our immediate reaction is to either deny or avoid it. But the philosophy of the Tibetan Buddhists is not to fear death, but embrace it and to think of death as the "crowning achievement" that symbolizes a life well-lived. Buddhists can view death in this manner because of their firm belief in reincarnation. These Tibetan Buddhists advocate that coming to terms with life and death is something that is easier to embrace through meditation. One Australian [study](#) supports this philosophy with research that reveals participants who were able to accept what couldn't be changed during their later phases of life experienced greater satisfaction.

- **Using Meditation to Heal** - As much as you may desire happiness, nothing is going to change unless you do something to change the underlying behavior and thoughts the create the negative habits that stop you from feeling happy. Buddhists are happier people because they heal themselves every day through meditation. It is through meditation that they are aware of what needs to change to be happier. Coming to terms with the source of the problems and then doing something to fix it is when change for the better happens. As your life gets better, you get happier.

- **Becoming More Patient** - They say patience is a virtue, but it is a virtue that has become lost in the modern world. Where everything is fast-paced, instantaneous, and constantly on the move, patience is no longer cultivated. We've forgotten how crucial patience is for our mental health. Buddha believed patience is one of the highest virtues we can attain. After all, he sat patiently in quiet meditation for days before he reached enlightenment. These days, we find it difficult to sit patiently for 30-minutes. We must have patience in our lives to help us deal with delays and difficulties without becoming upset. We deal with many things that are beyond our control every day, and if we can't avoid them, why do we continue to allow them to negatively impact our lives? Unhappiness is causing your suffering and when you're impatient, that suffering increases. Buddha taught his followers that the difference between what we want and what reality was is the reason *why we suffer*. Therefore, the only way to find peace was through managing our expectations.

- **Learning to Let Go of Unrealistic Expectations -** Unrealistic expectations will always be the cause of unnecessary suffering, and one of Buddhism's core tenets is learning to let our unrealistic expectations go. Buddhism calls for its followers to release their desire and expectation for a perfect world. Instead, find happiness is accepting reality for what it is. When you find something upsets you, asking yourself, *"What can I do to change this?"* will help you put things into perspective. If you can change it, do it. If you can't, then accept it.

What Does "Enlightenment" Mean?

The term enlightenment has been mentioned a few times already up to this point. It is a key term that is associated with Buddhism. Most people know that Buddha attained it and that Buddhists who have not attained yet, seek to do so. But *what does enlightenment mean to Buddhists?*

In English, *enlightenment* holds several meanings. During the 17th and 18th centuries, the *Age of Enlightenment* was about the philosophical movement that advocated science and reasoning over superstition and myth. In Western society, enlightenment is associated with knowledge and intellect. To the Buddhists, *"enlightenment"* is a concept that holds several meanings.

- **Satori -** Buddhism was first introduced to English speakers several decades ago through D.T. Suzuki's writings. Suzuki lived from 1870 to 1966, and he was a Japanese scholar who spent some time living as a Rinzai Zen monk. *"Enlightenment"* was a term Suzuki translated through the word *Satori,* a Japanese word taken from the verb *Satoru*. Translated, *Satoru* means "to know." Partially through Suzuki's influence, spiritual enlightenment was viewed as a sudden, transformative, and blissful experience and this notion became ingrained into Western culture. Unfortunately, this idea of enlightenment is misleading.

- **Bodhi (Theravada)** - In Sanskrit, the word *Bodhi* means "awakening" although sometimes it is translated to mean "enlightenment." Theravada Buddhists associate *Bodhi* to mean you have perfection your insight into the *Four Noble Truths* to end suffering. Those who have perfected their insight into these truths and abandoned defilements are *arhats,* and they have been liberated from the cycle of endless rebirth.

- **Bodhi (Mahayana)** - The Mahayana Buddhists see *Bodhi* as the perfection of wisdom. In this form of Buddhism, the enlightened one attains wisdom and understanding that we are all one, and the idea of being enlightened individually is nothing more than an oxymoron.

- **Vajrayana** - Vajrayana Buddhism is a branch of the Mahayana. The Vajrayana is the tantric school of Buddhism, and they believe that enlightenment comes all together in one transformative moment. They believe that hindrances and passions in life are not obstacles, but instead, tools that can be used to fuel our transformation and lead us to enlightenment. They believe this transformation can happen all at once in a single moment, and this inherent belief is rooted in *Buddha-Nature*. The *Buddha-Nature* is one of the founding principles of Mahayana Buddhism, symbolized by the infamous Lotus flower that many of us associate with Buddhism today. The *Buddha-Nature* is a tricky concept to define, but essentially it is the fundamental nature that exists within all living beings. The Vajrayana Buddhists believe that enlightenment is a permanent state.

- **Buddha-Nature** - Legend has it that when Buddha attained enlightenment, he said, *"It's remarkable! All beings are enlightened already!"*. Or something to that effect at least. The Buddha-Nature is a concept that forms a core component of practice in certain Buddhist schools. The Mahayana Buddhists, for example, believe that the Buddha-Nature in our inherent "Buddhahood," and this exists within all living beings. Therefore, since all beings already have this "Buddhahood" exists within all beings already, our responsibility is to *realize* enlightenment, not attain it. Master Huineng of China, the Sixth Patriarch of Ch'an (Zen), described Buddhahood as a moon that was obscured by the clouds in the sky. Our defilements and ignorance are the clouds, and when these clouds drifted away, the moon as it turns out, was there all along.

The Benefits of Enlightenment and Being Present

It is assumed that enlightenment can "solve our problems" and "bring about greater benefit." However, the Buddhists approach to life is to believe that the greatest benefit comes when you act (karma) without expecting any benefit at all. In short, to do all good things without expecting anything in return. You simply do it because you genuinely want to help or make a difference. "Expecting a benefit" for a good deed or action will only lead to disappointment when you don't get what you expected.

Enlightenment alone is not an absolute guarantee of happiness, and neither is being present. Instead, enlightenment and being present foster equanimity, a state beyond emotions. Enlightenment is not characterized by an experience (whether you feel happy or sad), but rather it is defined by your *awareness* of the experience. Awareness helps you grow, regardless of whether you perceived the experience to be positive or otherwise. Happiness, therefore, is a byproduct of equanimity. A person who is Equanimeous chooses their emotional state. They can choose happiness, or they can choose sadness (or any other emotion).

So, what does it mean to be enlightened and present? What benefits can we take away this state aside from the obvious benefit of being happier? Although the experience might differ based on the individual, the benefits you get from attaining enlightenment include:

- **Peace and Serenity** - An enlightened individual is at peace and feels serenity because they are no longer afraid of their unhealthy emotions. They are no longer afraid of the unknown and what they cannot control. They are no longer afraid of suffering, and they no longer hold attachment to material belongings. In that sense, freedom has made it possible for them to achieve what many of us have not yet been able to do. Find peace and serenity.

- **Kindness, Compassion, and Love** - An enlightened person is easy to spot because they show genuine care and compassion for those around them, even towards their enemies. Enlightenment has made them spiritually open to all beings and accepting of everyone.

- **Being Selfless** - Enlightenment connects you with the nature of your existence, and you are no longer the self-centered person you may have been because enlightenment has awakened you to the reality that we are all connected and dependent on each other for survival.

- **Emotional Stability** - When your ego is no longer needed as a validation for your existence, that's enlightenment. In the place of ego comes presence, understanding, and compassion towards others, and a greater tolerance for all living beings. Patience and understanding are now possible because enlightenment leads you to the realization that ignorance is the cause of your suffering.

- **Humility** - Being enlightened is a humbling experience once you awakened and know your place in the universe. An enlightened person no longer has any need to prove themselves to anyone, including themselves, and this knowledge allows them to live in a kinder, gentler, more peaceful manner the way most Buddhists do.

- **Power and Peace** - Being enlightened is powerful and peaceful at the same time. You know who you are, you know what you're capable of to remove suffering, and you're at peace with life because you're content with where you are and all that you have. You know what your strengths are, and enlightenment brings with it the knowledge of what you need to do to improve so things can get better. That is a very powerful combination that many are missing in their lives today.

Chapter 4: Teachings

Life has its bittersweet moments. On some days, you feel like you are on top of the world and so full of happiness you can't wipe the smile off your face. Other days things may not always go your way, and something could happen that sends you whole world crashing to a halt. That's the way it goes with the ups and downs of life. If there were no bad moments, we wouldn't appreciate the good times in life as much as we do.

Life may not always go your way, but that doesn't mean your happiness and peace have to be compromised. On the contrary, when you choose to follow observe certain core principles in Buddhism, specifically those related to suffering, karma, reincarnation, nirvana, and yoga, it can set you down the path towards a life that remains at peace no matter what happens around you.

Buddhism and Suffering

If only life could go the way that we wanted all the time. That way, we would always be happy and never have a reason to suffer or be miserable. Suffering, unfortunately, is inevitable, and that's why it was one of the first few concepts Buddha preached about to his followers, and he wrote: *"All that I teach is suffering and how to end it."* It seems discouraging, but to deny that suffering is part of life is only going to cause even greater suffering. Buddha taught his followers that if they chose to embrace the concept of suffering instead, it could empower them. Hardships are inevitable, but the way you choose to respond to those hardships is a choice that is always in your control. By changing the way you respond, you remove a lot of the self-inflicted suffering and emotional pain, the hardships or unpleasant circumstances may cause.

Buddha's solution to end suffering is laid out in the teachings of the *Noble Eightfold Path*. Even if you're not a devout Buddhist, you can still benefit from the Buddhist approach to alleviating pain, suffering, and misery. These core principles include:

- **Acceptance of Imperfections** - The more accepting and tolerant you are, the less stressed you will be. Acceptance of suffering may be a hard concept for some to grasp, but resisting or denying those emotions only traps you in that suffering longer than you need to be. Suppressing your emotions are never healthy and only leads to destructive habits that rob you of your peace.

- **Acceptance of the Present** - Nothing is permanent in our lives, and learning to live the present is the only way to find peace. Clinging to the past and worrying about the future will do nothing to change either of those scenarios. Resisting change (which is also inevitable) only causes frustration, resentment, anger, and sadness. Buddha taught his followers to learn to live by appreciating what currently exists, to immerse themselves in the present rather than struggle or resist against the impermanence of life.

Buddhism and Karma

Karma. A word most people know, yet very few understand its true meaning. In the Western world, *karma* is thought of as "fate" or the cosmic justice system. You get what you deserve. If you did something bad and something even worse happens to you, that's because you had it coming. That's not quite how the Buddhist see it, though. In Sanskrit, the word *karma* translates to mean "action." The word *karma* has a more specific meaning associated with it in Buddhism, and it is often used to describe our *willful action*. This means that what you choose to say, think, or do will set your *karma* in motion. Therefore, in Buddhism, *karma* is "cause and effect," not a cosmic justice system.

Living by the law of *karma* in the Buddhist way, it means that every action, thought, and word that you speak has consequences for you and those around you. Sometimes those consequences are unimaginable. It is your *karma* that shapes your life and the world around you, and by being mindful of the nature of your actions, you can *change your karma*. If you choose to live in a way that ignores this fundamental rule, where you don't care about the consequences of your actions, and you don't think before you speak, then you are responsible for the pain and suffering that is going on in your life because of that choice. If your actions, thoughts, and words are motivated by anger, hate, greed, or delusion, then you are responsible for sowing the seeds of your suffering. When your actions, thoughts, and words are motivated by wisdom, love, generosity, compassion, and a sincere desire to do good, you are creating a life of happiness and abundance.

Buddha described *karma* as volition because it was the motivation and intention behind your actions that determined what your *karmic* outcome would be. It is, therefore, every practitioner's responsibility to practice mindfulness and develop an awareness about their thoughts, emotions, and choice of words. Mindfulness was the skill needed to develop an awareness of what was going, and without this skill, we would never come to realize that we were creating our suffering. Be mindful of your actions, and you will create your peace and happiness.

Buddhism and Reincarnation, Nirvana and Yoga

Reincarnation is when a soul transmigrates from one life form into another. Reincarnation is not reserved for humans alone but applies to all living beings. Sometimes to non-living being too. Most Asian religions believe in the concept of reincarnation, and this belief is easily present in all the major religions in India, except for Islam. Buddhists believe that through reincarnation, they escape the *Wheel of Life* and attain *nirvana*.

The concepts of reincarnation that exist in Buddhism today were born from the Hindu concept of the same belief that first appeared in scriptures known as the *Upanishads*. Reincarnation is a never-ending cycle, and it is your *karma* that will ultimately decide what you are reborn as. The only way to escape the cycle of rebirths is through *nirvana*. Buddhist theology believes that within all of us dwells an "internal self" or "internal soul," and it is cosmic energy existing beyond reality. This reality does not need good deeds, prayers or *karma* to improve itself. The problem is, very few beings are tuned into this version of "self," and that is why they need prayers and good deeds to help them find their place in this word. Reincarnation is a way of getting one step closer to this soul.

The cycle of birth and death are continuous, and the aim is to get off the never-ending wheel to finally merge with our "Oneness." Meditation, yoga, and acts of charity are examples of methods that can be used to escape the wheel, and this belief is the driving force behind why Buddhists dedicate themselves to committing good deeds so they can attain a better position in their next life until they ultimately reach *nirvana* the way Buddha did. *Yoga* may be associated with relaxation, exercise, and stress relief in today's society, but it meant something very different during ancient times. *Yoga's* practices and rituals are infused within Buddhism, and both are aimed towards one purpose: *enlightenment*. Both Buddhism and *yoga* recognize suffering as a part of life, and that *freedom* from that suffering is also a very real possibility. *Yogic* practices used by many Buddhist practitioners go beyond trying to bend your body in various ways to test your flexibility.

The *Vajrayana* Buddhists in Tibet refer to any spiritual practice as *yoga*. Spiritually, *yoga* serves as a conduit for your energy. Your body is here as a resource so you can experience the physical nature of the world you live in. For the soul to communicate with your inner self, you need to walk the spiritual path, and *yoga* is the conduit that helps you get to your destination.

Say the word *nirvana,* and most people would associate the term with Hinduism first and Buddhism second. In both religions, *nirvana* talks about a higher state of being, although they view this state differently. Hinduism sees *nirvana* as the highest state of enlightenment a person can attain whereas, in Buddhism, *nirvana* is heaven, a place where you can finally be happy and at peace.

All Buddhists strive to attain *nirvana,* and its followers are encouraged to follow the *Four Noble Truths* and the *Eight Noble Paths* to attain enlightenment and bring an end to suffering. *Nirvana* can be attained through wisdom, mental discipline, and ethical conduct, and once you do, it is the ultimate peaceful, blissful state of mind. *Nirvana* means that the cycle of rebirth can finally stop because, like Buddha, you have at last transcended this state.

Rituals and Rites

Originally, Buddhism began as a path to attain enlightenment but without having to use priests, Gods, or any form of intermediaries to do it. However, as Buddhism spread, other religions began to absorb and merge their teachings with that of Buddhism and thus, the religion today is more ritualized than it was when Gautama Buddha started it. The one thing Buddha always rejected was the ritual animal sacrifice, and he adamantly rejected the sacrificial system in Hinduism. Instead, Buddha sought to encourage his followers to find other means of achieving salvation and instead of sacrificing animals, perform good deeds and services to others instead.

Only through wisdom, morality, and meditation can a follower walk the path towards Enlightenment. Several rituals that are carried out as part of the religion, worship, and meditation among them. A unique aspect of Buddhism is that that worshippers can come to the temples anytime they feel like it or when they need to pray for something special. In Christianity, there is the Sabbath day, a single day out of the entire week that is dedicated to going to Church to worship and show your devotion to God. Buddhism has no such equivalent. There is no Sabbath day, no presiding priests who will conduct a mass. As a practitioner, you can go to the temple any day of the week.

Followers of the religion can choose to do this either at home or to come and worship in a temple. Going to the temple, however, is not essential or mandatory. Buddhists who choose to perform the ritual at home set aside a small room or a small area of their home that serves as a shrine. A statue of Buddha is placed here together with an incense burner and some candles.

Because this religion has been absorbed by several others across cultures and various parts of the world, several customs and practices have evolved along with it. Even worshipping alone now takes on several forms. Some practitioners worship by meditating on Buddha's qualities and teachings, while others choose to worship and honor Buddha through offerings that are placed before his statue, images, or relics. *Theravada* Buddhists have a tradition where practitioners offer gifts to monks sometimes, although in general they are encouraged to devote themselves to good causes and to be good to each other. *Theravada* Buddhism considers monks the embodiment of Buddhist practices, and monks are tasked with the responsibility to spread and share the wisdom of the religion's teachings by setting an example.

The *Mahayana* Buddhism form of worship is through devotion to the *Bodhisattvas* and Buddha himself. Here, the worshippers may at times sit barefoot on the floor as they face Buddha's image and chant. As the worshippers sit, they may listen to the chanting of the monks and partake in it.

Practices have evolved to become varied throughout the different schools of Buddhism and the cultures that have absorbed it. Despite its variations, two rituals have remained constant to all Buddhist traditions. These two rituals have deep roots tied to the early days of the Buddhist community.

The First Basic Practice: The Veneration

The veneration is the act of demonstrating respect, meditating on Buddha's qualities or the giving of gifts to the Buddha or other saints, and *Bodhisattvas*. The first foci of this veneration took place after Buddha's death. By the start of the Common Era, the production of anthropomorphic images of Buddha began. These images were placed next to other relics of Buddha and served as veneration focal points for his followers. As time went on, devotion became diverse, but this veneration practice has continued to remain a central traditional component of Buddhism.

The Second Basic Practice: The Monks and Laypersons Exchange

After Buddha's death, monks became the embodiment of higher levels of spirituality, and they make themselves available in several ways to the laity. To improve soteriological conditions, the laity gives the monks material gifts that are meant to serve as offerings. Exchanges may be structured differently depending on the different Buddhist traditions, but the monks and laypersons exchange remains a central component of Buddhist ritual and practice.

The *Uposatha* Ritual

To understand the true essence of Buddhism, you need to practice it, and it only through practice that you can begin to appreciate the wisdom behind its teachings and understand why certain rituals are performed. Rituals become powerful when you immerse yourself in the experience completely in mind, body, and spirit. The many schools of Buddhism today have diverse and varied rituals, but there is an explanation for each ritual and why it is performed. Certain chants that you repeat, for example, are meant to help you gain merit. The meaning behind each ritual that is performed in Buddhism will unfold as you progress throughout the practice. No matter what the explanation may be though, the outcome goal of each ritual is the same. To attain enlightenment. Rituals are not the magic formula or shortcut to enlightenment. They merely serve as a tool to move you in the right direction.

As for the rites, ancient Buddhist tradition observes types of holy days that the *Theravada* countries (Sri Lanka, Myanmar, Thailand, Laos, Cambodia) within the Southeast Asian region continue to observe. These holy days are called the *uposatha*. Certain scholars believe that the *uposatha* days originated in the fast days preceding the *Vedic soma* sacrifice. Monks and laypersons are expected to fulfill their religious duties during these holy days. On the new moon and full moon of each lunar month and the eight-day after the new and full moon are considered the *uposatha* days.

During the *uposatha*, flowers are offered to Buddha's image. The precepts will be repeated; the *Pali suttas* will be recited, meditation, and a sermon by a monk will also be carried out for those who are present. Pious laymen make vows to observe all eight precepts during the *uposatha*, including the five precepts of not killing, lying, stealing, consuming intoxicants, and abstaining from sexual misconduct. As for the monks, their practice is to listen to recitations by one of their own about the rules of conduct in the *Vinaya Pitaka* during the *uposatha*. During this time, the monks may confess if they have violated any of these rules.

Depending on the sect, individual, and country they hail from, the daily specifics and rituals of Buddhist practice would vary quite considerably. For the most part, Buddhist monks continue to follow the *Vinaya* rules that were put in place by the early Buddhist centuries earlier. Monks also take on the responsibility of hundreds of vows that help to regulate their daily activities. They are required to behave with respect and decorum, and some temples even prescribe periods of intense meditation at various throughout the year.

Based on the ritual calendar, certain rituals are carried out based on the prescribed times while other rituals may be performed by request. These rituals can be carried out by the monks either within the temple itself or at the worshipper's home. This would vary based on the country. Some examples of the common rituals laymen might call on the monk to perform include the special blessings to succeed in certain endeavors. Monks in *Theravada* countries perform a daily ritual known as the Buddha *puja* where they place food, drink, flowers, or incense offerings before the altar or image of Buddha. This is briefly accompanied by a recitation. Some temples in *Mahayana* countries (Bangladesh, Nepal, Bhutan, China, Taiwan, Mongolia, Korea, Singapore, Malaysia, Japan, Vietnam, Indonesia) have a similar ritual.

Of all the rituals performed by Buddhist monks, the most common ritual is the one conducted for the dead. This includes funeral rites and the subsequent rites and rituals that should follow at different intervals after the person's death. The purpose of these rituals in Buddhism is to ensure the wellbeing of the deceased and to ensure their advancement into the afterlife.

The Anniversary of the 3 Major Events

Three major events happened in Buddha's life. His birth, his enlightenment, and his entrance to nirvana. These three major life events are commemorated by Buddhists countries around the world, although they may not be carried out on the same day.

- ***Theravada* Countries** - Observe all three life events in a single day known as *Vesak Day*. This day takes place in May on the full moon of the 6th lunar month.

- ***Mahayana* Countries (Including Japan)** - Observes these three life events on three separate days. April 8 is the day of birth in some countries. December 8th is the day of enlightenment. Nirvana is observed on February 15th.

In the *Mahayana and Vajrayana* traditions festival days that honor *Bodhisattvas* and other buddhas are observed too.

The Pilgrimage

The Buddhist community view pilgrimage as an important component of their practice and have been doing so within the first two centuries after Buddha's death. Early Buddhist history narrows down at least four major places of pilgrimage:

- **The Lumbini** - Where Buddha was born.

- **The Bodh Gaya** - Where Buddha achieved enlightenment.

- **The Varanasi (Deer Park)** - Where it was believed Buddha gave his very first sermon.

- **The Kushinara (Kushinagar) Village** - A location recognized as the place of Buddha's nirvana (final death).

The Bodh Gaya was considered the most important pilgrimage area in early history and continued to remain important throughout a large part of the history of Buddhism. After its downfall in India, Bodh Gaya was overtaken by Hindu groups, and it became part of a Hindu shrine. Only during the late 20th century when partial control was restored to the Buddhist did Bodh Gaya once more become a major pilgrimage site. Pilgrimages can be undertaken in any season.

Some Buddhists see pilgrimage as a way of fostering their development spiritually. Others undertake the pilgrimage to fulfill a vow they made. Others may simply see pilgrimage as a chance to travel and enjoy some of the most important locations in Buddhist history. Regardless of the reason, pilgrimages remain an important part of practice for a Buddhist.

Chapter 5: Practices You Can Implement in Your Life

Once Buddha attained enlightenment, everything changed for him. From that moment, he sought to do his best to enlighten as many people as he could and to help liberate them from the suffering of life. Buddha's daily routine is occupied with religious and spiritual activities unless he had to attend to his own physical needs. He was systematic, and he was methodical in the way he carried out his routine, and his inner life was focused on meditation and experiencing the *Nibannic* bliss. As for his outer life, that was dedicated to selflessly serving others.

For Buddha, his routine saw his day divided into five time-blocks or sections:

- **4 am-Noon:** It is said that Buddha would awake at 4 am, and as once he was ready, he would quietly meditate before looking at the world with compassion using his *third eye* (mental eye) to look for anyone that needed help. The day began by spiritually assisting all beings. The pure and the virtuous, like *Anathapindika,* would come looking to him for spiritual guidance.

- **Noon- 6 pm:** Buddha would take his place at the monastery as the *Bhikkhus* assembled before him to listen to the *Dharma.* He would provide spiritual advice and admonish disciples who were not following the path before retiring to his chamber to rest. In his chambers, he would once again use this *third eye* to look around the world to see who might need help. Through his preaching, illustrations, tales, and parables, his followers would be converted (although never by force, only by choice).

- **6 pm- 10 pm:** This time slot was specifically reserved for the *Bhikkus,* and Buddha would dedicate this time answering questions on the intricacies of the *dharma* and clarifying any doubts.

- **10 pm- 2 am:** During this time, the *devas* and the *Brahmas* would consult with Buddha about the intricacies of the *dharma*. The answers to their queries were recorded in the *Samyutta Nikaya*.

- **2 am- 4 am -** For the first hour, Buddha would exercise by walking around to relieve himself from any aches or strains that came with sitting all day. The rest of the time, before the entire cycle began anew, Buddha would spend sleeping for an hour before waking up, meditating, and radiating positive loving-kindness thoughts out into the universe towards all living beings once again.

Buddha spent the rest of his life in selfless service to others since achieving enlightenment. It is believed that he spent at least two hours a day (once in the morning and once at dawn) pervading the world with thoughts of loving-kindness and boundless compassion so he could bring as much happiness to as many people as possible. His life was one of voluntary poverty, seeking alms but making sure to never inconvenience others in doing so as he wandered from one location to the next spreading his teachings. Buddha was tireless in his efforts for the happiness and good of others, and before he entered *nirvana,* it is said that his last words were*:" Transient are all elements of being. Strive with earnestness."*

For the monks who live in a temple, the daily routine is one that is simple. The morning begins when the bells ring at 4.30 am (5 am when it's winter), and the monks would gather in the main hall of the temple for the morning chant and meditation. They would then enjoy a quiet breakfast in the dining hall before they begin their daily tasks. The tasks are of the day would depend on what activities are being run in the temple, and routines would change based on these activities. This would go on until lunchtime in the dining hall, after which the monks could choose to rest before beginning their tasks for the afternoon. Once evening rolls around, the monks would chant and meditate once more in the main hall, after which dinner would be served. Evening activities are flexible, and most monks bring their day to as end by going to bed at 10 pm. The routine would differ based on the various temple practices and schools of Buddhism of course, but the one similarity that all Buddhist monks share is that their life revolves around simplicity.

A Look at Your Routine as A Buddhist

Becoming a Buddhist is going to be life-changing. Your life will no longer be what it was, and in its place, a new and better routine will be cultivated. Undergoing any kind of major lifestyle change is challenging, even more so when you're doing it alone. Buddha passed into *nirvana* almost 2,500 years ago, yet his teachings are still going strong, and his followers continue to embody his philosophy, upholding his teachings. His wisdom is spread through qualified teachers of the *dharma,* and these teachers can serve as role models for the rest of us who want to take up Buddhism. As a beginner on this journey, getting a role model you can look to as an example you can emulate will be an immense help. Preferably someone who embodies all the qualities of Buddhism that you aspire too. The ultimate role model is Buddha himself, of course, but finding one that can guide you on your journey as a beginner will make it easier to overcome any obstacles you might face along the way.

Becoming a Buddhist means you need to begin taking responsibility for *creating* your life. You're not going to be living in the temple and waking up at 4 am each day like the monks do (unless you want to), but you need to be accountable for everything that goes on in your day from this point onwards. In keeping with the theme of simplicity, the routine of a Buddhist is, well, simple. It is about living with intention and gratitude for the most part, and this recurring theme begins from the moment they wake up in the morning. The typical routine of a Buddhist would look something like this:

- **When You Wake Up in the Morning** - As soon as you wake up in the morning, let feelings of absolute gratitude wash over you and flood you with happiness. You woke this morning healthy, strong, and capable, and that alone is something to be grateful for. If you have a roof over your head where you're comfortable and safe, you have a reason to be grateful. If you have food to eat today, you have a reason to be grateful. If you woke up this morning with the knowledge that you have family and friends who love and care about you, you have a reason to be grateful. A heart that is full of gratitude is a heart that is happy, and this is how you should aim to start your morning *every morning* from this day forward.

- **Set Your Intention** - The second step of your routine upon waking up is going to be setting your intention for the day. An intention could be what you want it to be. For example, today's intention might be *"I am going to make today meaningful and productive"* or *"Today, I will help anyone I see who needs help if I can."* Set your intention and do your best to live it out as you go about your day.

- **Meditating** - Buddhist monks begin the morning with meditation, and once you begin living life as a Buddhist, this will become a part of your routine too. Meditation is a good time for reflection and to begin the day in a calm fashion by finding your center. As you meditate, reflect on how your life is intertwined with the people that surround you. Their emotions and actions have an impact on us and vice versa, and that means we can choose the way we want to affect them. We can choose to be compassionate to spread feelings of love, warmth, and positivity. As you meditate, reflect on the intention you set for yourself earlier and use this time to strengthen your mental resolve to see it through.

- **Mindfulness** - The rest of the day is spent carrying out your usual routine, except this time with mindfulness. Be mindful of your thoughts, the words you speak, the way you act, the way you feel, and in everything that you do. Remain mindful when you're making yourself a cup of coffee, and when you're sitting at the desk working. Remain mindful when you're eating lunch and even when you're chatting with a colleague. Observe the emotions you feel throughout the day, and pay special attention to the negative or disturbing emotions you may encounter like anger, greed, jealousy, or frustration. Be mindful of your actions and whether you're acting impulsively, selfishly, or with bias and prejudice. When you catch yourself engaging in behavior that is not according to Buddhist teachings, use mindfulness to stop and reflect. Regulate your thoughts and actions before you say or do something that you will later come to regret. When you find yourself getting caught up in a cycle of negative emotions, use mindfulness to stop and think about the way these emotions are affecting you. Use mindfulness to recall the precepts that Buddhists are supposed to live by, and if your behavior is not what it's supposed to be, change it.

- **Meditating Again** - Buddhist monks begin their day with meditation, and they draw the day to a close in the same manner. Bring your day to a close by helping your mind, body, and soul unwind from the day's events by focusing on your breath. Thanks to science, we know for a fact that meditation does indeed change our brains. Not just the brain as it turns out, but our very nature too as Buddha himself learned firsthand. This practice is so powerful it led Buddha straight towards enlightenment. As you meditate, reflect on your actions throughout the day. *Did you do anything you wish you hadn't? Did your actions cause another harm? What can resolve to do tomorrow to make it better?* It is also important to reflect on the positive things that happened during the day. *Did you do something good for others? Did you help where* *you could? Did you act with genuine kindness and compassion towards those who needed it? What can you do tomorrow to continue gathering merit?*

A Day in The Life of a Buddhist

Buddhist monks seem to be so peaceful all the time not because they happen to be gentle, calm souls by nature. It is because they live their lives by a certain set of rules that the rest of us don't. A Buddhist's entire philosophy comes back around to one focal point. *How to reduce and minimize the suffering that they encounter.* Before beginning this journey into Buddhism, most of us would probably never even consider the possibility of embracing suffering, let alone welcoming the idea of death. Acceptance of these concepts is too difficult to comprehend because *why* would we choose to embrace what makes us miserable? Little did we realize that the resistance we put up was adding to our suffering all along, not protecting us from it as we thought.

The idea of being open to suffering instead of trying to do everything we can to avoid it, and not fearing death but rather accepting it, is an alien concept for many. In truth, this is the reason why Buddhists have attained the impossible. The highest state of happiness we all strive for yet can't understand why it continues to elude us. Esoteric Buddhist scriptures describe "Buddhahood" as having an undeluded mind. However, that state of mind is clouded by ignorance and defiled because of our emotions. Like the clouds that block the sun from view. To be as happy as the Buddhists, we need to live like a Buddhist by implementing the same practices they do. As a Buddhist, this is what life would look like:

- **You Uphold the Precepts** - The five precepts of Buddhism are your moral compass, and every good Buddhist strives to uphold its values in their everyday life. Sometimes the biggest change doesn't have to be a drastic move. The greatest change begins with a simple decision to start adhering to the precepts.

- **You Live Simpler** - Buddha was once a prince who had it all, and he gave it all up for a simpler life. A happier life. If a prince can let go of all that wealth, we can certainly let go of our need to cling onto the material possessions we believe is the source of our happiness. Buddha too had every opportunity to collect as much "stuff" as he wanted to, but he chose *not to*. Buddha realized long ago that the only true source of long-lasting happiness comes from within. Seeking it outside yourself is futile and will only end in either disappointment or more suffering. In Buddhism, a life of simplicity is a life that is happy.

- **You're More Giving** - One of the pillars of living a spiritually rich and full life is the awareness that a deeper sense of happiness is achieved when we selflessly devote ourselves to helping others. If there's an opportunity to help another, that's what we should all do. As a Buddhist, one of the principles you would learn to live by is how to cultivate a selfless attitude. Where the focus is less on all your personal troubles. When you learn not to sweat the small stuff, there's a greater sense of peace that goes with it. Not letting things bother you as much makes you calmer.

- **You Gather Your Merits** - Buddhists gather merits by cultivating compassion and through an intrinsic motivation to do good and help others in any way that they can. Those who regard themselves as Buddhists live a life where their offerings are "upward" while their generosity is "downward." This means that offerings made should be directed "upwards" towards the *sangha*, the Buddha's, objects where we take refuge, spiritual teachers, and towards the community of other practitioners. "Downwards" generosity, on the other hand, should be directed towards sentient beings. Offerings and generosity are practices that should be implemented daily since it is through acts of genuine kindness carried out with pure motivation and intent that we slowly start to gather our merit. The more merit you have, the fewer the hindrances and challenges you may face in this life.

- **You Approach All That You Do with Mindful Intelligence** - Instead of going through the motions on autopilot the way you've been doing all along, this time take a Buddhist approach to your endeavors by approaching it with mindful intelligence. Mindful intelligence means asking yourself the right questions that make you think about what it is you're doing. *What do I need to accomplish this task? Are my actions going to hurt others or do good? What information do I need to make the best possible decision? What qualities am I lacking in right now, and what do I need to do to change that?* Mindful awareness is a tool you need to start creating effective change within yourself and your environment. Intelligence is needed in *dharma* to be aware of our natural state and to keep the *bodhicitta* (enlightened mind) in mind. Many practitioners today are losing touch with the *bodhicitta* with the overwhelming responsibilities and stress of daily life. When it feels like too much is going on, you begin to wonder if enlightenment and peace are genuinely possible. It is when you approach all things with mindful intelligence.

- **You Become Part of the Community** - Buddhism may differ from other religions in a lot of ways, but the one similarity it shares is the strong sense of community. A community of practicing Buddhists is called a *sangha*, and they can consist of nuns, monks, lay-people who come together and unite for a goal or a purpose. Buddhist monks and nuns have always been involved in activities that can help to benefit the community. As a beginner, a good place to start getting involved in the community would be by attending classes that are held at the temple as your first step to getting connected with the local community. Many temples offer meditation, yoga and sutra lessons for those who may be keen to join in.

Successful Habits of Buddhist Monks You Can Adopt

You may not be a Buddhist monk or a nun, but that doesn't mean you can benefit from their habits. Clearly, they must be doing something right if they've managed to attain happiness living with so little. Most people can't even begin to imagine what life would be like without their mobile phones, fancy cars, and annual holidays abroad. Yet, the monks have something the rest of us want yet fail to achieve time and time again. They have mastered the secret to staying calm, focused, peaceful, and most importantly, *happy*. Where the rest of us complain, they express nothing but gratitude. Where we think about ourselves and our needs first, they selflessly devote their time and energy towards helping others and trying to make a positive difference in the world. How do they do what they do and *still* never lose that sense of happiness? That's a secret we would all like to know, and the answer can be found in the habits that they have.

These habits are practices that we too can easily adopt into our lives as part of our journey towards becoming a Buddhist. Like all habits, they are going to be challenging in the initial stages as you start getting used to them, but once they do become a habit, the benefits you gain will last you a lifetime.

Habit #1 - Decluttering You

Could you imagine devoting your life, your thoughts, and your actions towards the good of others? To be completely selfless and put the needs of others first before your own? Monks in several Buddhist circles have learned not to do things for themselves, but to do it for the good of the whole world. When they meditate, they do it for the sake of all the people in the world. When they try to achieve enlightenment, it is so they can reach their full potential and be in a better position to help those who may need them. They have decluttered themselves of any selfish wants, needs, or desires to make room for a more selfless attitude to develop. In doing so, they can focus less on their personal plights, and they don't sweat the small stuff anymore because they realize there are bigger issues in the world that need attention. This inner decluttering is a habit that you need to begin cultivating. Empty your mind, body, and soul of your old habits, so you can make room for the new ones.

Habit #2 - Decluttering Your Environment

Initiating change on the inside is a good place to begin, but you need to declutter your external environment too. 2,500 years after Buddha's death, his monks are still following in his footsteps by giving up all their worldly and material possessions. Decluttering the belongings down to the bare minimum and only what they need to survive. They say that everything a Buddhist monk needs to be happy will be enough to fit into a small backpack. This is how they have learned to let go of their attachment to earthly possessions that do nothing to contribute to long-lasting happiness.

Look around your home at how much you own. How many of these items can you say in all honesty that brings you immeasurable amounts of happiness? If you didn't have these items, would your life take a significant turn for the worse? Does the absence of these items increase your suffering? Clutter only distracts you from the present, and it makes it hard for you to appreciate the little things in life when you're distracted by an overwhelming number of non-essentials. Becoming more mindful begins when you declutter your external environment.

Habit #3 - Attaining Wisdom from the Elders

The relationship that Buddhist monks have with the older members of society are very different from the kind of relationship the rest of us have with the elderly. We're so busy running around trying to get our own affairs sorted we don't stop long enough to listen to the words of wisdom and experience that the ones who are older than us have to share. Among Buddhist monks and many Buddhists practitioners, the elderly are a source of wisdom, and they seek out the elderly for spiritual guidance to help them walk the right path. The older generation has a lot of experience and insight that can serve as incredible life lessons if only we stopped long enough to listen.

Habit #4 - Listen with Mindfulness, Not Judgment

Another hard habit to break out of is the ability to listen without an ounce of judgment on our part. Our brains are naturally wired to be judgmental towards others. Buddhists, however, believe that the whole point of human communication to teach u how to help ourselves and help others experience less suffering. Judgment and criticism are obviously not the way to go since in doing so, your actions are hurting others, and that goes against the precepts of Buddhism. Mindfulness is the key to listening and speaking without judgment. Mindfulness allows us to take in what someone is saying and evaluate it without being critical. The problem with our current method of communication is that we pre-plan our answers *while we are listening*. What mindfulness seeks to do is to simply listen and do nothing else.

Habit #5 - Understanding That Change Is the Only Law

To be accepting of change instead of resisting it, we need to understand that change is *the only law*. Buddhist master Suzuki once said that if we don't learn to accept the fact that everything changes, then we cannot find perfect composure. Change is difficult for us to accept, but unfortunately, that is the truth, and if we cannot accept this truth, then we will continue to suffer.

Habit #6 - Focus Only on One

A lie we have been living with for far too long is the belief that multitasking increases efficiency. That is a fallacy, and it has been scientifically proven that the human brain *does not cope* well when it has to multitask. Focusing on just one thing at a time is a key criterion of Buddhist philosophy, and that is how they remain present in the moment. No matter what else may be happening, focus on the present and commit your full attention to it. Focusing on one thing at a time gives you the ability to remain engaged throughout the task and because you'll be less stressed when you don't have multiple things you're juggling at a time; the result is greater peace and inner calm.

Habit #7 - Don't Control What You Cannot

Those who insist on controlling aspects of their life that are beyond their control will remain in a state of suffering. Learning to let go of what they cannot control is a large chunk of how Buddhist monks and laymen live their lives, and it is the reason why they remain calm while the rest of us continue to stress. Life is not always going to work out like you thought it would, and it goes back to the fundamental universal law again that all things change over time. The more you resist, the greater the suffering you bring upon yourself.

Habit #8 - Removing Your 3 Poisons

Three vices, in particular, must be removed from all our lives if we hope to live in greater joy and peace. Buddhists refer to these vices as the *3 poisons,* which were also mentioned in the earlier chapters of this book. The *3 poisons (hatred, greed, and delusion)* must be a habit that you break out of and leave behind as you begin your journey towards becoming a Buddhist. Overcoming these vices is going to take time, but it is an essential habit to remove to rid your life of suffering.

Chapter 6: Mindfulness and Acceptance Techniques for Anxiety and Stress

Mindfulness has become the latest buzzword and coping mechanism that many today are slowly turning to for help relieving their anxiety and stress. Mindfulness as a stress aid is "in fashion" these days, the "magic pill" to help us cope with the stress we face each day. Yet, not many are aware that this technique is derived from Buddhism's teachings of awareness and being present in the moment. It is more than a stress-reduction technique or a quick antidote to relieve the stress we feel. It is a *mindset* that helps you separate your stressful thoughts and overwhelming emotions that cause you anxiety.

Understanding Mindfulness

Jon Kabat-Zinn, American professor emeritus of medicine and renowned expert on the subject of mindfulness succinctly mindfulness as: *"Paying attention in a certain way, on purpose, being in the present and not being judgmental."* At its core, mindfulness is essentially your ability to remain fully present without being overwhelmed or too reactive to what's going on around you. You don't need to be a Buddhist either to begin practicing mindfulness because *everyone* is capable of it. It is a natural ability we possess, and one of the most overlooked tools we have readily available to help us cope with the everyday stressors we encounter with our daily routine. It calls on us to bring our attention and awareness to what we are directly experiencing at this moment.

Mindfulness, in a nutshell, is *Not focusing on what happened 5-minutes ago*, and *NOT* focusing on *what's going to happen 5-*

minutes from now. It is about what's going on *NOW*. Focus on what's happening right now. That's mindfulness, and we need to tap into our senses, thoughts, and current emotions, training our minds to pay attention to our surroundings if we hope to use this coping mechanism to overcome anxiety and stress. Buddhist monks have been doing it for over 2,500 years. Kabat-Zinn only began popularizing this concept in the United States sometime in the late 1970s. Today, everyone seems to be hopping on board the mindfulness train to enhance both their physical and psychological well-being.

Admittedly, this is not going to be easy for many. Being mindful is like opening your eyes for the first time only to realize you may not like everything that you see. Chögyam Trungpa, a Tibetan meditation master, once likened this process as undergoing brain surgery without any anesthesia. Or having to listen as insults are being hurled at you one after another. Being a silent observer is not always an easy thing to do. It may not be easy, but mindfulness is meant to help you learn how to handle and acknowledge these difficult parts of yourself (such as emotions, thoughts, and feelings) until you eventually come to a point where you're able to accept what is, and be at peace with it.

Where Do Stress and Anxiety Come From?

It is human nature to be afraid of what we don't know. We worry, and we get stressed or anxious when it feels like we are not in control. Everyone has a tendency to overthink sometimes, but for some people, they go through this more often, and it can severely impact their day. Some of these people who overthink could also have anxiety disorders. There is no clear reason as to why the process of overthinking happens, but one thing that we know for sure is that nothing good can come out of excess worry and overthinking except *even more* stress and anxiety than you're already dealing with.

Anxiety is a natural human response to stress. It is a feeling of fear or nervousness about what may or may not happen. The American Psychological Association (APA) defines anxiety as *"an emotion characterized by feelings of tension, worried thoughts and physical changes like increased blood pressure."* Being stressed and anxious can be triggered over common issues like financial problems, health issues, or work stress. It is also not uncommon to be afraid of certain things, like getting an injection, taking an airplane or encountering a wild animal. Intense fear can also lead to anxiety. Although different people are triggered by different causes of anxiety, everyone will experience anxiety sometime in their lives.

Anxiety and stress are not to be confused with fear. Fear is an immediate reaction to events or stimuli that is especially threatening. On the other hand, anxiety is less intense, and it is a more prolonged response related to anxiety-causing triggers. Sometimes, people tend to feel anxiety creep up on them without knowing why. The brain regularly manages our anxiety and our fear without interfering with our daily life functions. If there is a threat coming on, our brain helps us make sense of it, and it either amplifies or quells the fear and anxiety.

What Buddhists Do to Calm the Mind

One technique that mindfulness uses to cope with anxiety and stress is through *Mindful Meditation*. This practice encourages us to remain aware instead of dwelling in the past or dreading the future ahead of you. Through *Mindful Meditation*, awareness of your existing surroundings is cultivated. Rather than reflecting on what could be or maybe, you simply live in the moment without any judgment or overthinking.

Buddha's approach to mindfulness was through what is known as the *4 Foundations of Mindfulness* written in the *Satipatthana* sutras. It is said that Buddha himself laid down these four foundations more than 2,500 years ago, and even to this day it still serves as a quintessential guide for mindful practice for all aspiring and existing Buddhists.

The First Stage: Mindfulness of Anatomy, Body, and Elements

The first stage guides us toward being mindful of more than just the thought in our head or what is going on around us. In this first stage, we need to be mindful of the body, anatomy, and the elements that make us. Being mindful of your anatomy means understanding the intricacies of the human body system. Understanding how the internal organs work and all the other various elements that make us fundamentally human. Buddha's recommendation was for every practitioner to spend some time deeply contemplating and being mindful of their body.

Mindfulness of the elements is quite literally referring to our physical connection to the fundamental elements of earth, air, fire, and water:

- **Mindfulness of the Earth Element** - Refers to being mindful of our physical bodies. Do we feel grounded to the earth? If not, why?

- **Mindfulness of the Fire Element** - Are you paying attention to your body heat (or lack thereof)? Have you stopped to practice gratitude for the way that your body feels and how its temperature is healthy today, which then allows you to go about your daily routine unencumbered?

- **Mindfulness of the Water Element** - The simple act of paying attention to the fluids that course through your body is an exercise in mindfulness.

- **Mindfulness of the Air Element** - This refers to the body's respiratory system, which you might have already been paying attention to if you practiced your breathing techniques.

What Buddha was trying to accomplish through this teaching was to get his followers to realize the conditioned, selfless, and impermanent nature of the things that surrounded their lives and to help them realize by letting go wholeheartedly, that is when you begin to obtain your "highest truth."

The Second Stage: Being Mindful Towards Feelings

Traditionally, Buddha would refer to mindfulness as what he called: *"Being mindful of your feelings WITHIN your feelings.* Buddhism considers that the human body 6 basic sensors, and not 5 the way most of us have been conditioned to believe. The sense of sight, sound, taste, smell, body, and mind. Yes, the mind is considered your sixth sense in the Buddhist context. Remember the *3 Poisons* that were talked about in the earlier chapters? Well, as it turns out, mindfulness is the way of dealing with this unwholesome frame of mind. Feelings of pleasure could lead to attachment. Feelings of pain could lead to an aversion to negative emotions. Feelings of neutrality eventually end in delusion.

Feelings can be a scary prospect to deal with. It is easier to deal with emotions and feelings when they're positive and happy. When you're dealing with the less than pleasant ones, your first instinct will be to refrain or deny them. To be mindful of your feelings is the only path to liberation from suffering. When you experience negative emotions, you must use mindfulness to remove any attachment you may feel during the experience. Mindfulness keeps a watchful eye on the way we behave when confronted with these difficult emotions. To live in a way that is experiencing emotion without getting attached or avoiding them is the key to mindfulness. Easier said than done.

The Third Stage: Being Mindful of Consciousness

There are 52 noted "mental formations" know in Buddhism. Mental formations come with categories of their own, and the teachings about this are vast. To begin, though, all you would need is to start practicing consciousness, watching your emotions come and go. Acknowledge that you are mindful *when you are mindful*. By acknowledging that you are mindful (such as when you say: *I am mindful that I am reading this book now)*, this is when you begin practicing being mindful of our consciousness.

The Fourth Stage: Being Mindful of Mental Objects

Your perception is going to have a part to play in this mindfulness stage. Think about a flower. When you perceive these thoughts of a flower, you are creating an image of the flower in your mind. The flower does exist, and it is probably in front of you right now, but you still create an image in your mind of what you are experiencing anyway. The image that we create represents our perception. It consists of several ideas, concepts, and thoughts attached to it the mind. Then, what happens is the mind begins to "layer" over reality. This approach will almost always either positively or negatively distort the experience.

Buddhists monks and laymen have taken Buddha's wise words and teachings to heart. Buddhists monks have successfully mastered the art of calming the mind and increasing energy through a range of coping techniques that include regulated breathing, meditation, yoga, and by using one more technique. *Equanimity*. Picture how different your life would be if all those little ups and downs no longer stressed you out or caused you anxiety. If your brain could be trained not to suppress or react to the emotional triggers you feel. That's what equanimity can do.

Bhikkhu Bodhi, a *Theravadin* scholar, and monk described equanimity as: *"An evenness of the mind, Equanimity is unshakeable freedom and a state of inner equipoise that could not be unbalanced by loss and gain, dishonor and honor, pain and pleasure, and praise and blame.* Monks and certain Buddhist laymen have trained themselves to acquire the kind of equanimity that is needed to maintain a vigilant presence of mind, and that is how they have continued to maintain a mind that is calm and serene while simultaneously combining this with meditation and deep breathing. The answer to the question as to why monks seem to be calm and happy all the time without a care in the world is not because they are never affected by stress. It is because they have found a way to deal with it through mindfulness, awareness, and equanimity.

Equanimity is described as a psychologically stable and composed state of mind that is undisturbed by the experiences or exposure towards pain, emotions, and any other phenomenon that would ordinarily cause a great imbalance of the mind in others. It is one of the incredible, sublime emotions that are part of being a practicing Buddhist. This is where Buddhists begin laying the foundation for wisdom, freedom, radiance, compassion, and warmth. Buddha said that an equanimous mind was *"immeasurable, abundant, without ill-will, without hostility, and exalted."*

Chapter 7: The Diet of a Buddhist

Not all Buddhist traditions call for its followers to practice strict vegetarianism, even for the members of the clergy. Mostly, vegetarianism is associated with East Asian traditions from Japan, China, Korea, and Vietnam. The cuisine many Buddhists and monks in East Asian countries are influenced historically by Chinese Buddhism where being vegan or vegetarian is encouraged based on the *Dharmic* concept of nonviolence. Vegetarianism is recognized by other *Dharmic* faiths too, not just Buddhism alone. Taoism, Hinduism, Sikhism, and Jainism see monks and a small handful of believers practicing vegetarianism throughout the year. The rest of the religion's followers may opt to take on the vegetarian diet during special occasions or celebrations. Since nothing about Buddhism is forced, its followers can still exercise freedom of choice over their diet. If being a vegetarian is not something you can do, and forcing yourself is only going to add to your suffering, you don't have to do it.

Theravada Buddhists abide by the *Vinaya* dietary rules, and it is believed that Buddha was a follower of this dietary regulation too. Monks who follow the *Vinaya* diet plan would only consume food between the hours of early dawn and noontime. Originally, this dietary plan was designed to meet the needs of the 5th-century Buddhist community in India. The idea behind this approach to eating was to avoid causing the monastics and the laypeople any kind of aggravation. The *Latukikopama Sutta*, where this diet is mentioned, claims that Buddha did not allow his monastics to seek alms once noon had passed to avoid any danger they might encounter later in the day and to avoid inconveniencing others. Some *Theravada* Buddhists opt to follow the *Bhikku* diet for an entire day after each quarter moon. This is part of the *Uposatha* practice.

Dietary Regulations in Different Buddhist Sects

Most Buddhist dietary regulations are centered around the five precepts, which serve as a base guideline for how Buddhists live. Since the first precept is to avoid killing or harming any living being, many Buddhists try to avoid consuming meat where possible to abide by this.

Traditionally, *Theravada* nuns and monks would gather alms for food or eat anything that they were given, even if it was meat. The exception to this rule would be if the nuns or monks knew, saw, or heard that the animal(s) was specifically killed to feed the alms-seeker. In that case, consuming this meat was deemed karmically wrong and negative since this was an impure act. Some Buddhist laymen follow this same restriction. *Pali Sutras* talk about how Buddha refused to make vegetarianism mandatory despite the suggestion of a student to make it so for the monastic precepts.

In the *Mahayana* Buddhist tradition, by contrast, several sutras explicitly prohibit followers from consuming meat. This prohibition can specifically be found in the *Surangama* and *Lankavatara* sutras. The Japanese Buddhist sects, on the other hand, generally believe Buddha ate meat, and all the Japanese *Kamakura* Buddhist sects have relaxed the rules of the *Mahayana Vinaya*. As a result, vegetarianism is optional. As for the monastic Chinese Buddhist community, Vietnamese Buddhist, and most Korean Buddhism, vegetarianism is strictly adhered to.

The *Mahayana* and *Theravada* Buddhists believe that practicing vegetarianism is part of cultivating the *Bodhisattva's paramita*. As for Tibetan Buddhists, the difficulty in getting grains and vegetables within the country make it difficult, if not impossible, for compulsory vegetarianism. However, several leading Tibetan Buddhist teachers agree that whenever possible, vegetarianism should be followed.

Dietary Restrictions

Japan, China, Vietnam, and Korean *Mahayana* monastic specifically avoid consuming garlic, plants with a strong smell like shallots, asafetida, *Allium chinense* (Chinese onion), and mountain leek. These are called the "Five Acrid and Strong-selling Vegetables" or "Five Spices." Avoidance of the five is based on the teachings in the *Lankavatara, Surangama,* and *Brahmajala* sutras. The rule has evolved in modern times to now include vegetables from the onion genus and coriander. These modern restrictions are thought to have originated from the Indic region, and some Hindu and Jain believers still abide by this rule.

Some Taoists follow additional restrictions, although the list of plants to avoid is different from the list that Buddhists follow. A strict Buddhist practitioner does have certain restrictions in their diet if they can't abide by being vegetarian. Many Chinese Buddhists believe that beef, large animals, and exotic species should not be consumed. There's another dietary restriction that not many people may be aware of, and that is to avoid eating animal organs and innards.

Buddhists stay away from intoxicants like drugs and alcohol mainly because of the five precepts they abide by, but also because it affects their ability to be mindful and maintain a clear head.

Common Ingredients Found in a Buddhist Diet

Given its strong roots in East Asia where Buddhism is mainly practice, rice is a staple ingredient featured heavily in most Buddhist meals. This is often served in the form of congee (rice porridge) as part of their usual morning meal. Other common ingredients include noodles and grains, stir-fried or cooked vegetables in a vegetarian broth seasoned with various sauces.

Seasonings would come in the form of what was common in the local region. In Japan's monastery, seasonings of vegan dashi and soy sauce were the most common, while the curry is a prominent seasoning in Southeast Asia.

Traditionally, dairy, eggs, desserts, and sweets were not consumed, but it is permitted today, and it is sometimes served during special occasions like the tea ceremony (Zen tradition).

Eating Times

The eating times for Buddhist monks and nuns would vary from those of the laypeople. Ordinary folk don't necessarily have strict eating schedules they adhere to since the daily routine might change based on what you're doing for the day. We eat when we feel hungry, and sometimes, we indulge in food cravings that bring us pleasure.

For the monastics, food is thought of as medicine rather than pleasure. In the spirit of following the *Middle Path,* food is consumed by the monastic in sufficient quantities, enough to keep the body healthy and functioning. The *Katagiri Sutta* talks of how Buddha, when he was touring the region of Kasi once with several monks, said to them that he does not eat meals in the evening. Despite not taking his evening meals, he was aware that his health was good; he had no illness and lived comfortably with strength and buoyancy. Thus, he encouraged his monks not to consume an evening meal and be aware of how they too would still live in comfort with good health.

Consequently, it became a tradition for the monastics to only consume food during the hours of dawn to noon. Despite the adjustment difficulties at first, the monastics soon began to realize the benefits of controlled eating. When a monk or nun consumed food outside the timeframe, they're committing an offense known as the *Pacittiya*. To seek redemption, they would have to seek out a fellow nun or monk and confess their misdeed. The simple act of accepting responsibility serves to increase their sense of responsibility and duty. The *Vinaya* rules are not meant to punish, but rather to cultivate greater awareness and mindfulness when exercising restraint. There are exceptions to the rule, of course, like when someone is sick and in need of more nutrition to aid in their recovery.

Depending on the monastery, an approximate eating schedule of a Buddhist monk or nun would begin with breakfast in the morning and the last meal of the day by no later than 6 pm in the evenings. The predictability of the schedule allows them to better plan their daily activities and regulate their appetite. Mindfulness is practice during meal times as the monks and nuns eat in silence without distraction.

Are You Still Considered a Buddhist If You Eat Meat?

Abstaining from meat is not what defines you as a Buddhist; it is the way you live. Being a strict vegetarian does not make you a better Buddhist if you are still dishonest, selfish and without any compassion for others. A person who chooses to eat meat yet lives each day with mindfulness towards others, kindness, and generosity in their thoughts, actions and words are still a better Buddhist than the vegetarian.

Exercising for Good Health

At the end of a long day of preaching and teaching, Buddha would pace around the monastery to relieve his muscles from all that sitting. Today, the exercises that the Buddhist monastics perform would depend on the monastery they hail from. Some monasteries keep things simple, where physical exercise consists of cooking, cleaning, and carrying out your daily maintenance tasks. Yoga and meditation are also common exercise practices that monks and laymen perform on a regular basis.

Tibetan Buddhist monks, for example, start their morning with prostrations, where their palms will be folded and place at their heart, throat, and head. This symbolizes the purifying of their body, speech, and mind. They would then prostrate themselves on the floor, and they do this several times. These prostrating moves are like yoga, and they are meant to help cleanse their internal energy along with burning calories for greater focus. For the Tibetan Buddhists, this is their form of physical exercise. In the *Vajrayana* tradition, these monks are required to complete a minimum of 100,000 prostrations as part of their preliminary practice, although some practitioners choose to continue with these prostrations daily.

Bodhidharma, who founded Zen Buddhism, was a warrior prince, and he believed that exercise and physical activity is a means to discipline the mind by using the body. In several Zen traditions, stretching, yoga, meditation, mindfulness, *Qigong, Makoho,* and relaxation are the regular exercises carried out. Shaolin Temple monks, on the other hand, have a more physically demanding exercise regime that consists of martial arts and Shaolin Kung Fu.

Chapter 8: Meditation

A lot of religions that exist today include some form of meditation in its practice. Meditation is a process that can be enjoyed by anyone, and you don't necessarily have to be the most religious person in the world to reap its benefits. In Buddhism, meditation is an essential part of its practice, and two of the paths in its *Eightfold Path* encompass aspects of meditation.

Buddhism is a deeply spiritual practice, and it seeks to encourage its followers to get the most out of it by learning how to connect. Connect with themselves better, and to connect with the world around them in a deeply transformative way. If they succeed in doing this, they can attain enlightenment the way Buddha did, and meditation is one of the tools through which this goal is accomplished. The Buddhists were not the first people to practice meditation. Meditation has long been part of Hindu tradition before it became part of the Buddhist tradition after Buddha attained enlightenment.

How the Buddhists Do It (Types of Meditation)

As the years went by and Buddhism continued to evolve and grow, so too did the meditation techniques that were practiced. Mindfulness meditation, visualization, and loving-kindness meditation are some of the common practices today, although the different schools of Buddhism would approach meditative practices in their way. In Tibet, they favor visualization meditation, which might be accompanied by a repeated mantra used to focus the mind. The mantra in use would be one that embodies the truth of the religion's teachings. *Theravada* Buddhists tend to favor mindfulness meditation by focusing on their breath, body, feelings, and thoughts that move around in their minds as they sit in quiet contemplation.

Several meditation techniques have involved over the years, depending on the local culture in question. These are three of the most common methods:

- **Shamatha Meditation** - Shamatha translates to mindfulness, and *Shamatha* meditation is one of the most well-known forms of meditation in Buddhism. The focus of this approach is to cultivate equanimity, calm, and clarity for the practitioner, which ultimately leads to inner peace. When it is combined with *Vipassana* practices, this can eventually lead the practitioner to a spiritual awakening. *Vipassana* means awareness, and both the *Shamatha* and the *Vipassana* can be practiced by all, regardless of tradition or faith. It's not reserved exclusively for Buddhists alone.

- **Metta Meditation -** Also known as the loving-kindness, you'll find several variations of this meditative form too. Loving-kindness begins with the *Shamatha* before progressing into loving-kindness once the mind has become receptive and settled. One approach to carrying out this meditation is by directing thoughts and wishes of love, kindness, and wellbeing towards ourselves. From there, those wishes are projected outwards to the closest person or pet that may be within your vicinity at the time. As you progress deeper into the move, that love starts to flow towards all living beings no matter where they are or how we feel about them. Yes, this means wishing love and kindness even to those you may not like. This practice aims to radiate feelings of love outwards until the lines that distinguish between "me, my friend, and my enemy" become blurred, and we are all one. When we reach this state, what we are left with is simple, pure benevolence. Some practices invoke the use of mantras to inspire these feelings. A traditional Buddhist mantra for this type of meditation is: *May all living beings find happiness, and find the cause of that happiness. May they be free from all suffering, and the cause behind the suffering.*

- *Contemplative Meditating* - Buddhist teachings have some fundamental beliefs that they share, and practitioners are urged to reflect on these teachings through quiet contemplation. In other words, meditation. *The Four Thoughts that Transform the Mind* is one example of a well-known contemplative practice. The aim of contemplative meditation is simple. It gives your mind something to focus on and a reason to meditate, so you don't sit there for the next hour or two struggling to reign in your thoughts. Under the *Four Thoughts that Transform the Mind,* the four thoughts in focus are as follows:

    o Everything exists for a cause. Every action comes with consequences. Our actions could be more impactful than we think.

    o The choice to devote my energy to cultivating wisdom and compassion is my choice to make. I can choose to cultivate this power to benefit others.

    o Nothing in life is permanent. Everything changes.

    o Sooner or later, there will come a time when we are separated from our material attachments. Therefore, it is better to focus our time and energy on cultivating wisdom, compassion, and spirituality instead.

The Benefits

Buddhists gain more than just a sense of peace and calm through meditation. The ease of suffering requires keeping the mind and body healthy, and meditation is a natural way to do that. With regular meditation, life becomes a lot more peaceful, and it is easier to let go of attachment to the impermanence. Life is full of stress, and the busy mind will never be quiet unless we *do something* to intentionally calm it down.

The 17th Gyalwang Karmapa, a Tibetan Buddhist teacher, once said that meditation was a way to awaken trust within us. Awakening this trust was a way to realize that we are beings full of compassion and wisdom, something we may forget when we're too caught up with everything else that goes on in our lives. Meditation is meant to cultivate a greater awareness within us and provoke us down the path towards profound realization.

For Buddha, meditation was ultimately an essential tool that he encouraged his followers to adopt to help liberate themselves from suffering. After his death, Buddhism spread across the world, far and wide and along the way, embraced several spiritual strengths and characteristics of the local culture. Every form of Buddhist meditation technique that exists today has arisen from Buddha's teachings about the cause of suffering, happiness, and the nature of existence.

Even if relaxation is not your goal when you start this journey, it is still going to be part of the result regardless. The term "relaxation response" was coined by Herbert Benson, an MD researcher at Harvard University Medical School in the 1970s conducting research on a group of subjects who practiced a technique called transcendental meditation. Ever since then, research about meditation and its many benefits (including relaxation) have documented just how beneficial this practice can be for the nervous system. Lower blood pressure and heart rate, better blood circulation, less stress, less anxiety, better feelings of wellbeing, and lower cortisol levels are just the beginning of what meditation can do for the mind, body, and soul.

As for Buddhists abiding by the Buddhist philosophy, meditation's ultimate benefit is its ability to liberate your mind from the attachment that you've formed to the things you cannot fully control. To be liberated is to be "enlightened."

Meditation and Prayers Are Different

On the outside, it may seem like they are the same. But meditation and prayers are two distinctly different approaches. The former involves petitioning God, a higher power, or a deity, worshipping and praying to them to seek assistance or offer gratitude. The latter focuses on guiding the practitioner through a transformation.

Meditation's Biggest Challenges

There are several obstacles a new practitioner might face when they're just starting out. One such obstacle is the misconception that you're either going to be very good at it, or you're going to be terrible. There is no good and bad when it comes to meditation. Thinking that you're a failure is a false belief because the truth is if you can pay attention to the way you breathe, then you can meditate.

The second challenge encountered by new practitioners is not knowing how long they should meditate. Ask most Buddhist teachers this question, and they will tell you that the length of time does not matter. It's not about how long or how little time you spend meditating, what matters is what you get out of it at the end of each session. The length of time you can commit should not be a major concern that stops you. Any amount of time spent meditating is good. The secret to success is trying to work out what you can comfortably manage and make that a habit.

One of the more obvious challenges is the physical discomfort that new practitioners experience. Looking at Buddhist monks, you might imagine that they are the perfect picture of calm and comfort, but even they sometimes experience discomfort while they meditate.

Mastering the Basics: How to Begin to Meditate

The first thing you need to as you begin to prepare to settle into your meditative session is to sit in a comfortable, balanced position. Your back should be as straight as possible, but not to straight to the point of tension. The idea is to be comfortable enough that your body can mentally and physically relax, and discomfort is only going to make it harder for you to focus. If you need to, use a chair or a pillow for additional support. Your spine's natural curve should allow the air to move freely through your diaphragm.

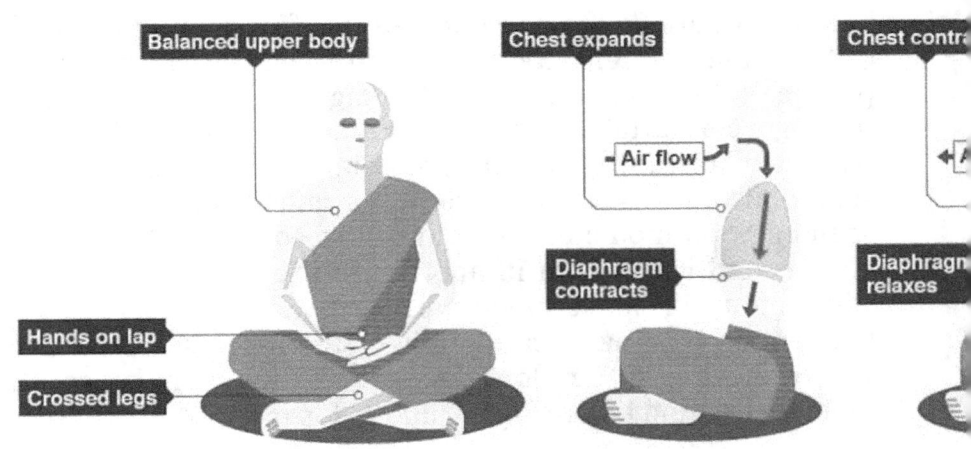

Image Source: BBC UK

The next step is to close your eyes. Begin to bring your attention and awareness to your breath as it drifts in and out of your body. Let the movement of your breath be one only thing that your mind is focused on as your eyes remain closed. At the start, you might feel as though your mind is like a rushing river, and your thoughts are just racing past you in a flurry. It can seem impossible to try to calm your thoughts and get them to slow down, but the key is to take it one step at the time. With each breath in and out, release one thought or worry from your mind.

Pick a time to meditate during the day that works best for you. Whether it is done in the morning, noon, or night does not matter. What matters is *the timing is what works best for you.* This should be a time when you feel ready to spend several minutes in quiet, contemplative silence. Although the monks and many Buddhists laymen find it helpful to begin their day with meditation, you don't have to follow this routine if it does not work for you. You might be one of those who find it helpful if you could clear your mind and relax before bed. In that case, meditating in the evening would suit you best. The time of day and the length of the meditation does not matter.

It is important to ensure that you're not too tired before you begin meditating. Tiredness makes it difficult to attain the level of focus and concentration you need to get the most out of this practice. Wear comfortable clothing before you begin. Like finding a comfortable position to sit, uncomfortable clothing that restricts your movement and breathing can be a distraction. You should also perform this session in a quiet room where you can spend several moments alone undisturbed. Turn off your mobile devices and leave them in another room. Even the vibration of your phone in silent mode will serve as a distraction. If you happen to be living with a family or roommates, let them know you would like to be alone for a few minutes and respectfully request they don't disturb you unless it is urgent.

How to Perform the Shamatha

To carry out the *Shamatha*, this is what you need to do:

- Start by sitting in a comfortable position, ensuring you're not experiencing any discomfort or hurting your back in any way.
- Begin observing your breath. Don't manipulate or try to change it, simply breathe normally except this time, pay attention to how the air flows with each breath.

- Should any thoughts pop into your mind during this time, acknowledge them, but don't engage. Observe, but then let go.

The *Shamatha* forms the basis of your meditative practice. This is where you get your start as a beginner. From here, it is easy to progress towards other types of meditation as you slowly advance in your practice.

The Advanced Meditation Technique that Frees You from Suffering

The *Mahamudra* is an advanced Buddhist meditation technique that first began in India before it began flourishing in Tibet through Buddhism. This technique is meant to teach you how to naturally rest within the essence of your mind. The *Mahamudra* is so advanced that in Tibet, it is one of the highest forms of meditation. It is practiced in the School of Kagyu, which is regarded as one of the four main Tibetan Buddhist schools. Since this practice is meant to free you from suffering, it emphasizes what your *personal experience* is in meditation. Some masters even claim that the *Mahamudra* is so powerful because it combines all the other meditations to form one ultimate and complete, powerful practice.

To practice the *Mahamudra,* you need to look at your nature curiously through a self-inquiry process. Imagine you rediscovered yourself for the first time, and you're honing in on the little details to get a clearer, overall picture. The more curious you are, the greater the inner discover. You need to be genuinely relaxed during this process and fine-tune your awareness about every situation in your life. That awareness will lead towards acceptance and appreciation of who you are.

Begin in the same position you would with the *Shamatha* and empty your mind. As you close your eyes, you should feel a sense of calm and control. Maintain good posture, keeping your back straight, so you can regulate your breathing. The power of your breath is an important component of this move. Next, in the seated position, assume the *lotus gesture* or *mudra,* with your thumbs touching each other as the left-hand cups the right. Your hands should form the shape of an oval like the image below:

Image Source: Buddha Weekly

The nature of this gesture is meant to symbolize oneness. Our hands are always busy, always on the move, either handling tasks or texting on the phone. People hold onto their phones far too much, and as such, their hands are always busy. The only time our hands are at rest is when we're asleep. Once you've got your hand placement just right, breathe through your nose as you keep your eyes closed halfway. Your head should be tilted slightly. Make sure your posture is feeling comfortable, and don't force yourself to do anything you can't handle.

Allow yourself to free your mind as you drift deeper into this meditative state. The *Mahamudra* believes that the answer to what the truth of our nature lies in who we are before we fabricate a false identity for ourselves. The face that we present to the rest of the world, hoping they will like us by hiding part of our true nature. When you stop *creating* an image for yourself and accept the truth of who you are. Seeing yourself for who you is the only way to remove the ignorance that has been the cause of your suffering all this time. Quite simply, the truth shall set you free.

Chapter 9: What You Didn't Know About Buddhism

As simple as it seems on the surface, Buddhism is a practice that is a lot more complex than we think. It is easy to think that we know all there is known about the religion through the research we do on the subject. Yet, when we scratch and dig a little deeper beneath the surface, we might be surprised to learn that there are still things about it we didn't know.

5 Things You Didn't Know About Buddhism

Every religion has an interesting story to tell, and Buddhism sheds light on these five things that you might not have known about the practice:

1. There's No Official Standard of Buddhism

It is a religion practiced by millions around the world, yet there is no "official" standard of belief when it comes to Buddhism. That is what sets it apart from all the other religions in the world today. Unlike Christianity and Islam, the other two major religions, Buddhism does things its own way, and it is not always standard across all practice. Some schools of Buddhism, for example, have monastic life as part of its practice while others don't.

2. Sometimes Buddha is Depicted Fat, and Sometimes He Is Skinny

The idea that Buddha was fat before he began his journey to become the Buddha, we know today is incorrect. The story is that

Buddha slimmed down during his fasting days before he attained enlightenment is a myth. The reason there are different depictions of Buddha is that *there is more than one Buddha*. The historical version of Buddha is Siddhartha Gautama.

Image Source: Learn Religions

The "fat" version of Buddha originated from a character out of the old folk talks from China, and his legend began to spread across Asia. In China, he is known as "Budai." In Japan, they call him "Hotei." In time, the "fat" version of Buddha (also called the Laughing Buddha) became associated with *Maitreya,* a Buddha from the future age.

3. Buddha Sometimes Has an Acorn on His Head and Here's Why

Buddha is not always depicted with an acorn on his head, only sometimes. Legend has it that the individual knobs seen on his head are really snails who voluntarily positioned themselves there to cover Buddha's head. It is believed they either did this to keep him warm or to help him cool off. However, this legend is a myth.

Image Source: Learn Religions

The artists of Gandhara created the very first images of Buddha. Gandhara was an ancient Buddhist kingdom, and today its location within an area now referred to as Pakistan and Afghanistan. In those ancient times, the artists were heavily influenced by Roman, Persian and Greek artwork, and thus, the reason why Buddha is depicted with curly hair that is tied in a topknot. Apparently, this hairstyle was stylish at that time. Eventually, depictions of Buddhist art slowly moved into China and other parts of East Asia where the curls became stylized knobs, and the original topknot style became a bump on his head that is supposed to represent wisdom. If you're wondering why his earlobes are so long, it is because during his time as a prince he used to wear heavy gold earrings that caused his earlobes to elongate.

4. Not All Buddhists Wear Orange and Yellow Robes

Contrary to the stereotype, *not all* Buddhists dress in orange and yellow robes. It is the *Theravada* monks from Southeast Asia who generally wear orange, although the shade of orange could vary. Sometimes the colors could be burnt-orange, and sometimes it resembles more of a yellow-orange shade. Some monks even dress in robes that look like tangerine orange.

Yellow robes are worn by the Chinese monks and nuns on formal occasions. In Tibet, the robes are maroon and yellow, while in Japan and Korea, the colors of the robes are either black or grey. However, some ceremonies may require the monks and nuns to wear several color varieties. The saffron-colored robes are a legacy among the first Buddhist monks. There's an interesting story behind the choice of color. It is believed that Buddha told his chosen disciples upon their ordination to make their robes using "pure cloth." At that time, pure cloth meant no one else wanted it, and the monks and nuns had to search through rubbish sometimes for used cloth. Sometimes, these pieces of cloth were used to wrap corpses that were decaying. Or the cloth had been discarded because it was saturated with too much pus. The discarded cloth was rendered unusable by others and had to be boiled for a significant period. To cover the stains and the odors coming from the cloth, the monks and nuns added all sorts of vegetable matter to the boiling water. Anything from bark, flowers, roots, and fruits. Leaves from the jackfruit tree was a particularly popular choice.

This was back then of course. Today, nuns and monks make their own robes from cloth donated to them.

5. There Are No Women Buddha's

There are no statues that look like female Buddha's, but if you were to ask the question: *Are there any female Buddha?* The answer would depend on what you meant by the term "Buddha." That's because, in some *Mahayana* schools, the term "Buddha" refers to the fundamental nature of all living beings, both male and female. If you go by that context, then "Buddha' could be a representation of both males and females. An old belief was that only men could enter nirvana, and although this was expressed in certain *sutras*, the *Vimalakirti Sutra* has directly debunked this notion.

Amazing Zen Buddhist Stories That Teach Us About Life

There's a rich history of storytelling to be found in the Zen tradition. What makes these stories even more compelling is how much they can teach us about life, and the lessons we learn from them. Like some of these Zen stories below, for example, each with its own nugget of wisdom that teaches us about life:

Story 1 - Suzuki Roshi's Lesson on Impermanence

One day, a student asks Suzuki Roshi during a lecture: "Suzuki, I've been listening to you for years, but I still don't understand. Could you describe Buddhism in one phrase?". Suzuki replied: "Everything changes."

Suzuki Roshi's story of impermanence serves as a reminder that if we continue to hold onto things, we will continue to trap ourselves in the cycle of suffering.

Story 2 - The Horse and the Boss

A horse was galloping down the road, and it seemed the man on it had somewhere important he needed to be. A man standing by the side of the road shouted "Where are you heading?" to which the man on the horse shouted back "I don't know, ask the horse!".

This short but impactful story reminds us of our habits. The horse represents our habit and unless we become intentional about our actions and mindful of our habits, we won't be in control of the horse.

Story 3 - It's Not Always About Following the Rules

Ekido and Tanzan were traveling a muddy road together and the rain was falling. As they turned the bend, they saw a girl in a silk kimono who couldn't cross the intersection. Tanzan offered to life the girl in his arms and carry her over the mud. Ekido remained silent until they reached the temple. Finally, when he could bear it no longer, Ekido exclaimed: "Monks can't be seen with females! That was dangerous why did you do it?" Tanzan replied, "I left the girl already, why are you still carrying her?".

This story reminds us that sometimes, to do the right thing, you need to break the rules. The important thing is that you do what's morally right, let it go and then move on.

Story 4 - When It's Time to Die

Zen master Ikkyu was clever, even when he was a boy. Ikkyu's teacher had an antique and rare teacup that was precious and Ikkyu broke the cup and was extremely perplex. He held the pieces of the cup and tried to hide it behind him when he heard his teacher approaching. When he saw his master, he asked: "Why do people need to die?". The master explained that it was the natural order of things, and everything had to die. Ikkyu revealed the teacup to the master and said: "It was time for your teacup to die".

Death is something many of us fear, but Buddhism reminds us that although it is inevitable, it is not tragic. It is simply the way that life goes, and we shouldn't let that fear stop us from living the best life we can in the present.

Famous People Who Follow Buddhism

In every religion's history, there are a handful of influential people who have made an impact either on the religion directly, or on its culture and influenced others to follow suit. Buddhism is no different.

The 14th Dalai Lama

Image Source: Beliefnet

The 14th Dalai Lama is probably the most recognizable face associated with Buddhism today. Born Lhamo Dhondup in July 1935, the Dalai Lama was recognized by the age of two as a reincarnation of the previous Dalai Lama. He began his education at the monastery when he was six and has learned and lived in Tibet until he was forced to flee in 1959 when Chinese troops invaded Tibet.

Today, the Dalai Lama goes by the name Tenzin Gyatso, and he has spoken on several occasions about various teachings of Buddhism, the welfare, and plight of Tibet. For many westerners, he has become synonymous with Buddhism and has single-handedly increased the Western world's understand and growing interest in the religion. The Dalai Lama has also spoken about several social issues and collaborated with other faith leaders in several interfaith dialogues.

Thich Nhat Hanh

Image Source: Beliefnet

Born in Vietnam in 1926, Nguyen Xuan Bao, better known as Thich Nhat Hanh, is a spiritual leader, author, peace activist, and poet. He had a significant role to play in uniting Buddhism with the Western world and has founded six monasteries, more than 1,000 *sanghas,* and dozens of centers for Buddhist practice. Hailed as the "Father of Mindfulness," Thich founded local communities that came together to practice mindfulness. He has also been hailed as "The Other Dalai Lama." Martin Luther King, Jr. called Thich "an Apostle of nonviolence and peace." Thich has actively lobbied against the war in Vietnam and has led the Buddhist delegation during the 1969 Peace Talks in Paris.

In November 2014, Thich suffered a stroke one month after his 88th birthday. However, he returned to Plum Village, where he currently resides after a year of intensive rehabilitation.

Steve Jobs, American Entrepreneur

Image Source: The Verge

The former CEO of Apple was a lifelong practitioner of Zen Buddhism, a branch of the *Mahayana*. From an early age, Jobs was a spiritual seeker and even traveled to India in search of spiritual wisdom.

Adewale Akinnuoye-Agbaje, British Actor

Image Source: Wikipedia

Actor Adewale Akinnuoye-Agbaje is a British actor and a Nichiren Buddhist. He is also a member of the Soka Gakkai International Buddhist association. Nichiren Buddhism is part of the *Mahayana* family and follows the teachings of Japanese Buddhist priest Nichiren.

Chow Yun-Fat, Hong Kong Actor

Image Source: Pinterest

Despite the characters he plays on television, actor Chow Yun-Fat is a peace-loving Buddhist. He once said during an interview that in real life, he hates violence, but he has no choice because it is his job.

Tina Turner, Retired Singer, Songwriter and Actress

Image Source: Wikipedia

Turner was raised as a Baptist but later became a Nichiren Buddhist and credited its spiritual healing that helped her endure the difficult times in her life. Turner refers to herself as a Buddhist-Baptist, and in a 2016 interview stated that she considers herself a Buddhist. Turner has been practicing Nichiren since 1973 after being introduced to the religion by a friend.

Conclusion

Thank you for making it through to the end of *Buddhism for Beginners*, let's hope it was informative and able to provide you with all of the tools you need to achieve your goals whatever they may be.

It is a religion that has inspired millions around the world through the lessons it teaches us about letting go of the things we cannot control and embrace the inevitable parts of life we have been fighting so hard to avoid all this time. In the end, the world that surrounds us is a product of our own actions. That's what Buddhism wants us to learn because the knowledge that we are directly responsible for what goes on around us is also the key to breaking out of the cycle of suffering.

The path to happiness and peace is a road that can be traveled by anyone who is willing to embrace what goes with it, as Buddhism has taught us. Happiness lies in simplicity and balance, without leaning towards one extreme or another. At its core, Buddhism's main message always goes back to kindness, compassion, peace, and mindfulness. If everyone in this world could walk the Buddhist path, we would all be living in a world filled with harmony and peace.

Finally, if you found this book useful in any way, a review on Amazon is always appreciated!

www.ingramcontent.com/pod-product-compliance
Lightning Source LLC
Chambersburg PA
CBHW050319010526
44107CB00055B/2313